$\mathscr{S}$EARCHING FOR MRS. OSWALD CHAMBERS

*One Woman's Quest to
Uncover the Truth about the Woman behind the
Most Celebrated Devotional of All Time*

Searching for
Mrs. Oswald Chambers

MARTHA CHRISTIAN

TYNDALE HOUSE PUBLISHERS, INC.
CAROL STREAM, ILLINOIS

Visit Tyndale's exciting Web site at www.tyndale.com

TYNDALE and Tyndale's quill logo are registered trademarks of Tyndale House Publishers, Inc.

Searching for Mrs. Oswald Chambers: One Woman's Quest to Uncover the Truth about the Woman behind the Most Celebrated Devotional of All Time

We gratefully acknowledge the Wesley Center Online, Northwest Nazarene University, Nampa, ID 83686, for granting permission to include the quoted material on the Holiness Movement in chapter 7.

Designed by Beth Sparkman

Edited by Susan Taylor

Library of Congress Cataloging-in-Publication Data

Christian, Martha.

  Searching for Mrs. Oswald Chambers : one woman's quest to uncover the truth about the woman behind the most celebrated devotional of all time / Martha Christian.

     p. cm.

  Includes bibliographical references.

  ISBN-13: 978-1-4143-2332-9 (sc)
  ISBN-10: 1-4143-2332-8 (sc)

  1. Chambers, Biddy, 1966-   2. Chambers, Oswald, 1874-1917.   3. Chambers, Oswald, 1874-1917. My utmost for His Highest.   I. Title.

BR1725.C43C47 2008

269′.20922—dc22
[B]   2008004642

Printed in the United States of America

14 13 12 11 10 09 08
 7   6   5   4   3   2   1

To

*K*athleen.

Righteousness
will bring peace.
Yes, it will bring
quietness and
confidence forever.

ISAIAH 32:17 (NLT)

ONTENTS

$\mathcal{I}$NTRODUCTION

My Utmost for His Highest is almost a household word in many Christian homes. Spoken into being during the early 1900s by Oswald Chambers, a man of great spiritual strength and stature, his words have comforted generations of souls seeking a closer walk with Jesus. O. C.'s faithfulness to his God, his purity of purpose that the answer lies with Jesus (not beliefs about Jesus), and his delightful way of explaining how to lay hold of the truths of God have instructed, informed, and inspired those who have come to meet the Christ who lived in Oswald Chambers.

Eager for spiritual growth, anxious for God to get me in his grip, and having heard of the godly wisdom in *My Utmost for His Highest,* I bought a copy of the book for myself.

Opening the front cover, the foreword caught my eye. Hurriedly, I scanned the page and noticed the initials *B. C.* located at the end. Like many others, I suppose, I glossed over those initials without a thought, immediately moving to the first page, marked "January 1."

A year passed, during which I studied the solid teachings of Oswald Chambers. Referring to my Bible often, I prayed to know God as he had known him, to come to realize that Jesus (not what I believed about Jesus) was the key to faith.

During that first year, I struggled, felt my shame at my slow growth and lack of charity, knew a joy that rose above life's problems, and looked forward to another year for more of the same.

When the time rolled around to begin a new year with *My Utmost for His Highest,* I again opened the book, but slowly this time. The foreword read, "It is because it is felt that the author is one to whose teaching men will return, that this book has been prepared, and it is sent out with the prayer that day by day the messages may continue to bring the quickening life and inspiration of the Holy Spirit.—B. C."

Instead of hurrying ahead to the first page, "January 1," I stopped dead in my tracks.

Who was "B. C."?

ROLOGUE

Women were important to Jesus. He honored them, set them free, and raised them to a high calling for their lives.

In a time when women were considered unimportant property, slaves to service, and items to be kept under lock and key in the back rooms of society, Jesus came.

Jesus loved and cared for his mother, Mary. The divine love and loyalty he demonstrated to his friends Mary and Martha during the illness and death of Lazarus lifted them, curing their crisis. Jesus bridged the chasm of racial discrimination when he spoke to the woman of Samaria. He broke the bondage of her life, offering her life eternal instead.

Jesus cared about women. He set the example of sacrificial love, to the point of his death on the cross, and he provided the path for women to be set free.

Oswald Chambers, best known for the words found in *My Utmost for His Highest* and often considered a spiritual giant and evangelical prophet, loved Biddy Chambers, his wife, with Christlike love. He cared for her, prayed for her, and joined his life with hers to serve God.

In 1916, he wrote a note to his wife saying, "When I consider how completely and nobly you have foregone all quiet civilised influences that other women have and have been living a literal hand-to-mouth existence all transfigured by your great love for me and Him, I must bow my head in dedication and say God bless thee!"

Biddy was clearly the kind of woman of whom the

book of Proverbs says, "Her husband praises her" (Proverbs 31:28, NLT).

These words from her husband must have caused Biddy's spirit to soar above the trials of a life of physical hardship. That note, tucked under her pillow when her husband had to be away for a night, lightened her load by cheering her heart.

Already serving God, Biddy Chambers was lifted to the very throne of God by her husband. His love for her set her free to abandon her own life to the life of Christ in her.

She lived the powerful life of Christ's love flowing through her to everyone around her.

One year after receiving that treasured note, Mrs. Oswald Chambers became a widow. The sudden death of her husband after only seven years of marriage left Biddy with a young daughter to raise alone, facing a future of uncertainty thousands of miles away from home. Biddy Chambers accepted these trials with the certainty of faith in Jesus Christ.

The Word spoke to her: "Bring my soul out of prison, that I may praise thy name: the righteous shall compass me about; for thou shalt deal bountifully with me" (Psalm 142:7, KJV).

Out of the bounty of God comes *Searching for Mrs. Oswald Chambers*.

—Martha Christian

You must give some time to your fellow man.
Even if it is a little thing, do something for those
who have need of a man's help, something for
which you get no pay but the privilege of doing it.
For remember, you don't live in a world all your
own. Your brothers are here, too.

—ALBERT SCHWEITZER

$\mathscr{F}$aith

ZEITOUN, EGYPT
1917

> *[Jesus] said, "This sickness is not unto death, but for the glory of God, that the Son of God might be glorified thereby."*   JOHN 11:4, KJV

Biddy Chambers brushed a wisp of hair from her forehead and tried to grasp the events leading up to her husband's death. For a moment she sat alone on a rough wooden bench in the devotional hut in Zeitoun, Egypt. She could still see him speaking. Tired but relying on God's strength, he offered the light and hope of Jesus Christ night after night to war-weary soldiers who needed comfort during the terrible First World War.

The cross that marked his grave stated simply "Reverend Oswald Chambers, Superintendent, Y.M.C.A., 15TH November 1917, Age 43."

Has it only been a week? Biddy pushed down the tears that threatened.

She knew she had to go on. The soldiers, the volunteers, and their faithful friends believed her to be strong. They were used to her steady stride, her infectious laugh, her generosity, and her ability to endure the desert heat. Other than her long, dusty skirts and windblown hair, her tidy appearance was always the current fashion of high-neck collars, and her brown hair was swept up away from her face and piled on top of her head. Even in the driving wind and blowing sand, Biddy Chambers remained an English lady.

Looking around the familiar hut, she could hardly realize Oswald Chambers was gone. When he was alive, she hadn't noticed the irregular, rough surfaces of the walls. Did the end of his life mean that the work was over? "We need him," she whispered to the empty room.

Biddy remembered how Oswald had always comforted her: "Poverty in brain and body and heart is blessed if it drives us to his fathomless resources."

It was true. But sometimes, through the long hours of work involved in feeding soldiers and caring for their daughter, Kathleen, Mrs. Oswald Chambers felt overwhelmed, even when her husband was beside her.

"Mrs. O. C.?" The voice seemed to come from a long way off.

"Yes? Oh, yes, what is it?" Biddy stood and turned to smile at the soldier, whose face wore an expression of deep loss. He held his hat in his hands.

"Will you be talking to us tonight, then?"

"Oh, yes. Yes, I will."

"Thank you, then." The war-weary Australian looked much older than his twenty years. Grief does that to people. "I'll see you then."

"See you then," Biddy replied. Oswald was in the presence of God. He would want her to continue the work in Egypt. She had to "do the next thing."

"What were Oswald's words to me?" She tried to recapture the sound of his voice, but she could not.

She did, however, have something he had written to her not long after they arrived in Egypt: "When I consider how completely and nobly you have foregone all quiet civilised influences that other women have and have been living a literal hand-to-mouth existence all transfigured by your great love for me and Him, I must bow my head in dedication and say God bless thee!"

How could she, a young widow thousands of miles away from her home country of England, carry on the work of helping people? What would she say to the assembled soldiers who loved her husband's message of God's order in the midst of chaos? "'God's order in the haphazard,'" she said aloud. Her head felt heavy, and her shoulders sagged. Her heartbreak seemed too great to endure. As if living a bad dream, she sank down on the wooden bench and pressed her fingers to her forehead.

The soldiers were used to Biddy's steady stride, her infectious laugh, her generosity, and her ability to endure the desert heat.

Biddy knew that God's grace was sufficient. His Word had spoken to her and sustained her through the days of Oswald's illness. *This sickness is not unto death, but for the glory of God"* was the message she felt God was telling her.

She could continue because God's Word said, "As I was with Moses, so I will be with thee. . . . Be strong and of a good courage" (Joshua 1:5-6, KJV). Biddy reached for her ever-present notepad and quickly wrote down that promise.

"Mama?" Little Kathleen was suddenly standing beside her. Her daughter's faith in God gave her strength and comfort. Kathleen did not question God or his way. She believed Jesus always knew best.

Biddy put her arm around her daughter and pulled her close.

"Yes?"

"What does 'scallyway' mean?" Kathleen patted Biddy's arm.

Mrs. Oswald Chambers smiled. "Our Little Flower of God," she whispered against her four-year-old's soft hair. Biddy pulled Kathleen onto her lap. "First of all, it is pronounced 'ska-li-wag.'" She bounced her little one on her knee.

"Why did Daddy call me that?"

"Because he loved you very much."

"But what does it *mean*?"

"It means it is time to get some supper ready. How many guests do you think we will have tonight?"

"Lots. We always do!" Kathleen hopped onto the rough floor.

"Well, then, go wash your face and tidy your hair. Your ribbon is all lopsided." Biddy gave her daughter a gentle push toward the door.

Suddenly serious, Kathleen turned questioning eyes toward her mother. "If Daddy is with God, how can he be here, too?"

The question tore through Biddy like a knife. Standing up, she straightened her long skirt and said softly, "We'll talk about that later, but it is possible." She smiled. "With God, all things are possible."

Mrs. O. C. was a good mother: strong, kind, and happy. She would not fail her daughter. "I'll be along in a minute."

Once Kathleen had left the hut, Biddy allowed a few tears to fall and then noticed a fly whisk on the reading table next to her. *Was this the one he always carried?*

She constantly fought with the insect population. The flies were especially annoying. Now Oswald would no longer surprise her by suddenly swatting them. She picked up the whisk and put it in a safe place.

Biddy remembered how Oswald had always comforted her: "Poverty in brain and body and heart is blessed if it drives us to his fathomless resources."

Later, with dinner over and "Scallyway" Kathleen put to bed for the night, Biddy returned to the empty devotional hut. She felt restless. She had managed to give a message of hope to the men who longed for home and family and who might die on the battlefield the very next morning.

Biddy recalled how she had approached the place where the soldiers sat on wooden benches. She had spoken to them outside in the open air that night because of the desert heat. As she walked over to them, she had prayed quietly for God to be her strength and shield. Then, taking a deep breath, she straightened her skirt, walked briskly to where Oswald would have stood, and looked at her audience. The love of God flowed through her eyes to them, and she spoke from her heart: "When Jesus said to believe in him, it might seem like climbing a high tower where one must hang on or fall. But in reality, to believe in Jesus means we have a place of strength, and joy, and security. Belief *in* Jesus, not beliefs *about* Jesus, is what Oswald would have told you if he were here tonight. We have to go forward. As we trust God for each day, he will give us the provision of strength. We can be at peace because the light of Jesus Christ will lead us toward that perfect day when there are no more wars, or rumours of wars, and where the lamb will lie down with the lion."

There in the hut alone, Biddy recalled the meeting that night and how she had watched their faces at full attention.

"It was as if a veil had been drawn aside," she said softly.

The years at Zeitoun, Egypt, where Oswald had offered all he had out of his love for God, would have lasting impact, because God's Word would endure forever.

And Biddy knew without a doubt that Oswald's solid foundation of teaching faith in God was not wasted when he spoke the words from Philippians 2:17: "If I be offered up on the sacrifice and service of your faith, I joy and rejoice with you all" (KJV).

Oswald had not doubted God, his methods, or his way. An eagerness to do God's will, as God made it clear, would carry those boys through the days in this life.

And maybe by tomorrow, she thought, *into the next life.* Her heart ached not only for her husband but also for the young men, many still in their teen years, who would face the ultimate test on the battlefield—death.

Holding the Bible Oswald had loved brought her comfort. Touching the books he read gave her a sense of peace. Finally alone, and away from eyes that tried to search her soul, she gathered her thoughts.

She was surrounded by people who counted on her now, as they had counted on Oswald ever since he had arrived in Egypt. *Was it three years ago?* Biddy tried to keep her mind from wandering.

"How can anyone be so alone?" She spoke quietly. One of the things she missed most was sharing the events of the day with her husband. How they had laughed together!

It had seemed to happen suddenly, his sickness, but then, time ran together just now. One day he was fine, walking briskly around the compound. The next, he was not feeling well. Then he had stomach pain. "Probably nothing," he had assured her. "Just something I ate. Your cooking," he teased, and he gave her a hug. But when he could barely get out of bed, even stoic Oswald knew something was wrong.

"Should you go to hospital?" Biddy tried to keep her tone light and her manner offhand.

"The hospital is needed for the wounded," he replied. "I just need a bit of rest."

Gizeh Red Cross Hospital was next, however. Biddy had trusted God while the doctors removed her husband's appendix. Since the men back at the camp in Zeitoun were busy praying for Oswald's recovery, she had accepted it when the medical team said the surgery was a success.

A noise outside the hut startled her, and in spite of herself, Biddy jumped. Fanning her face, she reasoned, *Nothing at all.*

"Nothing at all" was what she thought would be the

outcome of Oswald's hospital stay. Still, she had stayed with her husband at the hospital and watched over him. And she prayed.

Biddy had clung to the words from John 11:4: "This sickness is not unto death, but for the glory of God, that the Son of God might be glorified thereby" (KJV). The familiar verse of Scripture seemed deeply impressed on her soul as she went through the long, weary days of Oswald's illness.

Now, however, sitting alone in the hut, she was uncertain. Oswald was needed, not only by the war-weary soldiers but by others, too. "*I* need him," she sighed. This time the tears flowed freely.

How is it, then, she thought, *that he died?*

Biddy knew the medical diagnosis—a blood clot in the lung. Then another blood clot formed, and she watched Oswald fade before her eyes. More prayer.

Oswald had miraculously improved, and little Kathleen was allowed to visit him.

Weak as he was, Oswald had opened his eyes and said, "Hello, Scalawag."

"That's where she heard 'scallyway.' Now I remember." Thinking out loud brought him closer.

He didn't look like himself because he had lost so much weight, but Kathleen didn't seem to notice.

How could Biddy ever forget the way her husband had tried to smile when Kathleen told him all about her donkey back at the Y.M.C.A. camp at Zeitoun?

The visit had ended all too soon.

Biddy knew Oswald was in God's presence. She realized that God was in control, but now she faced a future of uncertainty as a widow and as a single mother in a time when women were usually protected by their husbands—or left to deteriorate on their own.

Biddy tiptoed to the sleeping quarters to check on her daughter. Kathleen didn't stir when Biddy fixed her bed-covers and removed her favorite doll from her grasp. Unable to rest, she walked slowly back to the devotional hut. She could feel God's Spirit there, but she could not breach the barrier between heaven and earth.

Picking up Oswald's Bible again, she sank onto a hard chair. "Now he is gone. I must face it."

Biddy knew that history would record his passing as November 15, 1917, at the age of forty-three. She did not realize, however, that her own life would have an impact on future generations, even into the twenty-first century and beyond. The grave was temporary. The impact of a life of service to Jesus Christ is eternal.

Oswald had often mentioned that, rightly related to Jesus Christ, one life could be of great service to God. Biddy was unaware that hers would be one of those lives.

She opened the Bible and read, "Bring my soul out of prison, that I may praise thy name: the righteous shall compass me about, for thou shalt deal bountifully with me" (Psalm 142:7, KJV).

The Word spoke. Biddy Chambers listened.

$\mathscr{F}$uture

LONDON (ENGLAND)/
BRITISH COLUMBIA (CANADA)
1994

To You, O LORD, I lift up my soul.   PSALM 25:1

Somewhere in London, some poor man or his relatives may still wonder why an unknown woman in North America kept calling in September 1994. The message she left was always the same: "Please have Miss Chambers phone me back."

Undaunted by the lack of response, I continued to phone every Chambers in England. Most of the long-distance operators were very patient. I even exchanged a recipe for chicken soup with one young lady who seemed to have a bad cold.

I found that most of the Chambers-type people seemed to live in and around London. Like a miner searching for riches during the gold rushes of the 1800s, I plowed ahead without thought to inconvenience. I would let nothing stop me, not even a drink of water when I felt thirsty. *At least I don't have to wear hiking boots and carry a heavy pack,* I thought.

The difference was that I was looking for gold of a different kind, not the gold that glitters and gleams when fashioned into precious jewels or has purchasing power. *No,* I reasoned, *I'm looking for a faith that is finer than any gold fashioned by man, just like it says in the Bible: "These trials will show that your faith is genuine. It is being tested as fire tests and purifies gold—though your faith is far more precious than mere gold. So when your faith remains strong through many trials, it will bring you much praise and glory and honor on the day when Jesus Christ is revealed to the whole world"* (1 Peter 1:7, NLT).

Just as those early miners forsook the comforts of home to reach the Yukon, I felt called to my duties.

It's a good thing I don't have to climb mountains or fight off grizzly bears! I did allow myself to munch on a soda cracker at that point. I knew in my heart, however, that anyone who really followed Jesus Christ wholeheartedly would suffer, because faith must be refined in the crucible of affliction.

After all, the disciples paid a heavy price, as well as early Christians who were burned at the stake or thrown to the lions. Then we must not forget the saints and martyrs down through the years, or missionaries around the world, or people who die suddenly, or are crippled, or lose a child. I was getting off track again, so I dialed another long-distance number.

My quest had begun some years before, in 1983, when I began studying the life of the virtuous wife as outlined in Proverbs 31. Endeavoring to live that way myself, I searched everywhere to find a real-life role model for Christian women in the modern world. I knew from talking to my

friends and going to church and Bible studies that many
women aren't completely satisfied today, no matter what the
television commercials say about how easy it is to "eliminate"
dirt and dust without actually cleaning.

Then, in 1993, I came across a well-known book titled
My Utmost for His Highest. It lay on my night table for a
couple of days before I had time to open it. Then one day,
after completing the day's responsibilities dealing with
family, work, cooking, and mopping up from supper, I
eagerly planted myself in a chair and opened the book. It
was a whole year, however, before I noticed the initials *B. C.*
at the very beginning.

The foreword noted that the daily readings in *My Utmost
for His Highest* originated in the early years of 1900 but that
the author, Oswald Chambers, had died in 1917. I checked
out the copyright to find out when it was published.

How can the book be copyrighted in 1935? I wondered.

Hurrying to my desk, I grabbed my calculator (math was
never my best subject—I got through advanced algebra by
doing extra credit).

"Okay," I muttered, tapping out the figures, "approxi-
mately 1917 from 1935 equals eighteen years." That got me
nowhere.

It was a mystery to me. "And one needing to be solved!"
I announced to the cat lazing about on a nearby chair. I
pointed my finger forward the way a commander leads his
army during a charge. I could feel the excitement and thrill
of figuring out the puzzle before me. And that's when I
became serious about my venture. The cat, named Sebastian,
yawned, stretched, and turned over in disinterest.

I pushed the calculator away and drummed my fingers
on the writing pad. *What about those missing years? And*

why the initials B. C. but no name? They couldn't have been Oswald's, or the initials would have been O. C.

I knew that the writing was powerful, especially since former U.S. Senate chaplain Richard C. Halverson had said in the introduction that the teaching in the book kept him on track and that only the Bible had influenced his life more. I guessed from the 1935 copyright date that Chaplain Halverson might have written the foreword after Oswald was no longer on this earth. But then the initials would have been *R. H.*

It has been said that the best friend of the writer is the question why.

Since I had written three books and some magazine articles, I felt I could consider myself a writer.

Here goes, I thought. *Why?*

After adjusting my chair and dusting off the top of my desk, I put pencil to paper and began a list of questions: First, who was this person? *Why* was there no name? So ended my list.

"Obviously, I won't find that one out," I murmured in disappointment.

To give my brain, and my expedition, some rest, I moved on to a few household duties, baked some cookies, took a phone call from a friend, and did a little dusting. My intellect, however, refused to let it go.

I need more diversion, I thought, grabbing my car keys.

Since I needed groceries, I decided to table my questions and get a look at the world outside. Blue sky always made me happy. *That will put the whole thing out of my mind. It could be, as they say, "a wild goose chase," whatever that means.*

Heading down the stairs and out to the carport, I changed my focus from "find Chambers" to "find peace."

I got behind the wheel of the car, fastened my seat belt, backed out of the driveway without hitting the garbage can left in the middle of the road by my next-door neighbor, and headed toward town.

I shoved my reverie into the background, concentrated on driving, and promised myself that I would think about the mystery later that evening, when I'd completed everything on today's calendar.

Later, the errands completed, the dog and cat fed, and the house quiet, I realized my question was not *why* but *who*?

"Now we're getting somewhere," I said, quickly jotting "Find Who" on a scrap of paper.

Another week went by before I thought about *B. C.* again, because although my children were grown, I still kept in constant contact with them by telephone; I had my teaching schedule to maintain; and then, of course, the dog and cat required attention. I also took time to enjoy a colorful sunrise, a delightful display of rose to pink to light blue, and later, a not-so-impressive sunset.

"Thank you, God, for the heavens you have created," I whispered to the darkening sky, "and for the Light of the world, Jesus Christ."

It was September 1994 when the idea hit me to start "gold digging." Since the beginning pages of *My Utmost for His Highest* referred to London, I decided to call England and find out what I could.

I reasoned that the *C* from *B. C.* might stand for *Chambers,* so I went through several operators on both sides of the ocean in order to narrow down the options. After several attempts, I discovered that Mr. Melvin Chambers, who was not related to Oswald Chambers or his wife, would not return my calls. I still had no answer as to the whereabouts of anyone who had anything to do with *B. C.*

Finally, a circuitous route lead me to the telephone number of a Miss Kathleen Chambers, who, I hoped, might be the daughter of Oswald Chambers.

Impatiently, I tapped my fingers while I waited for the operator to connect me.

Then a woman answered. "Hello?" Her well-modulated tones and crisp speech belied what I later learned was an incredibly warm, loving heart.

"I'm really sorry to bother you, but I'm looking for someone by the name of Chambers."

"Yes," the voice responded.

"I think this person might have something to do with Oswald Chambers."

"Yes."

"Anyway, I want to thank you for speaking with me. I've been trying to find the right Chambers for several weeks now, and I'm pretty certain that Melvin isn't the right one."

"Yes."

"So." I cleared my throat. "Can you hear me all right, across the ocean, and all?"

"Yes."

I felt uncomfortable but decided to plunge right in. "Would you happen to know anything about Oswald Chambers?"

"Yes."

"Great! I've heard his daughter is alive and living in England, and that is why I'm calling you." I paused to collect myself and then continued. "You see, I've been reading a book that was written by him, but it is strange because there are initials at the front that just say *B. C.*"

"Yes."

"Am I keeping you from something?"

"No."

"Oh, good, because I know it isn't the same time there as it is here." I felt silly. *Why did I start this?*

"Yes," she patiently replied.

I lost all hope that this elegant lady would ever believe I was sane, but I blurted out the reason for my call anyway. "Would you happen to know anything about a minister who was named Oswald Chambers who lived a long time ago?"

"Yes." I thought I heard her chuckle. "He was my father."

Suddenly speechless—which is unusual for me—I contained my excitement and quickly continued. "Well then, maybe you would know what the letters *B. C.* stand for in the front of the book *My Utmost for His Highest.*"

She replied, "*B. C.* stands for *Biddy Chambers.* She was my mother."

"Oh! You must be Miss Kathleen Chambers!" I responded.

"Would you like to tell me who you are?"

I told her I was a writer searching for information about godly women, and more specifically, the answer to the question Can anyone actually live like that?

We spoke for more than an hour, and I took notes as fast as I could.

Miss Kathleen Chambers actually took the time to tell me stories about her mother, Mrs. Oswald—Biddy—Chambers, called "Aunty Biddy" by many who had crossed her path.

I couldn't believe my ears!

Biddy Chambers, the "B. C." I was looking for, *was* the

quintessential godly woman outlined in Proverbs 31. If one looked in a spiritual dictionary under the heading "Godly Woman," one would find *Biddy Chambers.*

Biddy Chambers kept the flame of faith in Jesus Christ burning. She lived what she believed, and others saw Christ in her eyes. The reflection of the light of Christ shines in the faithful ones who follow the path of the Cross, and Biddy Chambers mirrored the love of Jesus Christ. According to Kathleen, scores of souls have spoken of meeting her and finding new direction.

Jesus said, "You are the light of the world—like a city on a hilltop that cannot be hidden. No one lights a lamp and then puts it under a basket. Instead, a lamp is placed on a stand, where it gives light to everyone in the house. In the same way, let your good deeds shine out for all to see, so that everyone will praise your heavenly Father" (Matthew 5:14-16, NLT).

As I listened to Kathleen, I realized that Mrs. Oswald Chambers was the spirit, soul, and substance of godly femininity, and I wanted to find out who she was, how she lived her life, how the Spirit of Jesus Christ carried her, and how she let the Light of Life shine through her in everyday, practical activities.

From all I could discern, she lived her faith, demonstrating it each time she welcomed a stranger into her home or soothed away the tears of a child or sat up late into the night transcribing, then typing, the words spoken by her husband. Hers was a calling of the highest magnitude. The interesting fact to me was that she wasn't interested in herself. I decided her name should have been Humility Chambers.

I knew I had discovered a treasure more precious than gold. True, Biddy Chambers had lived in a world unknown to me, before cars and computers; but compared to the woman described in Proverbs 31, she qualified as "modern." In any case, I was captivated and captured by the life of Mrs. Oswald Chambers. I had to know more.

The next day, while driving my modern automobile down a nicely paved street, I began to wonder: *But that was then, and this is now. What about modern Christian women? Can we carry that same Christlike attitude?*

Over the next couple of weeks, I spent most of my time in research.

I had read some-where that the life of Oswald Chambers flashed across the sky like a meteor that lit the darkness briefly and then disappeared. From what Kathleen had told me in our initial conversation, it could be said of Biddy Cham-bers that her life twinkled steadily, like a star, beckoning all to look upward to the cross of Christ. It reminded me of Psalm 19:1: "The heavens declare the glory of God; and the firmament sheweth his handywork" (KJV).

Biddy Chambers, the "B. C." I was looking for, was the quintessential godly woman outlined in Proverbs 31. If one looked in a spiritual dictionary under the heading "Godly Woman," one would find Biddy Chambers.

I didn't care about the long-distance telephone charges. I couldn't believe how kind Kathleen was. The only child of Oswald and Gertrude "Biddy" Chambers was taking her valuable time to speak to me, a stranger, and lead me into the most thrilling adventure of my Christian life. She was a living legacy.

In the same way that a river flows from its source to its final destination, the story I was about to discover began in the past and continues flowing into an unknown future.

I decided to follow the stream.

THREE

*R*eflection

EGYPT
1917

Now we see through a glass, darkly; but then face to face: now I know in part; but then shall I know even as also I am known.   1 CORINTHIANS 13:12, KJV

Crying could not empty Biddy's heart of pain. The tears she shed over losing Oswald could never begin to moisten the unending sands of Egypt where she now found herself left alone with their little daughter, Kathleen.

That November 1917, sitting on a hard folding chair in the devotional hut in the horrendous heat, she knew faith was the answer. Not just any faith, but the same abiding assurance she had shared with Oswald, that nothing could separate them from the love of God. Jesus is the way. *All I have to do is follow him.*

At the reading table, Biddy carefully opened her Bible. She was comforted when the Word spoke to her heart: "Such trust have we through Christ to Godward. Not that we are sufficient of ourselves to think any thing as of ourselves; but our sufficiency is of God" (2 Corinthians 3:4-5, KJV).

She remembered that Oswald always said it was impossible for God's child to be weak in God's strength. Sitting quietly, she felt the love and peace of Jesus Christ lifting her above her circumstances.

"If we walk in the light, there can be no darkness," she whispered softly.

She knew that to gain light for each step, she must obey God at every turn. She could almost hear Oswald telling the soldiers each night in the devotional hut to "walk in the light, as he is in the light." The price was complete surrender to God. The reward? The peace that passes all human understanding given freely to God's children. *Even in the face of death,* she thought.

Mrs. O. C. remembered the words of the hymn she had chosen for Oswald's funeral. Written by Charles Wesley in the 1700s, the message still seemed appropriate:

> *To the hills I lift mine eyes,*
> *The everlasting hills;*
> *Streaming thence in fresh supplies,*
> *My soul the Spirit feels.*
> *Will he not his help afford?*
> *Help, while yet I ask, is given:*
> *God comes down; the God and Lord*
> *That made both earth and heaven.*
>
> *Faithful soul, pray always; pray,*
> *And still in God confide;*
> *He thy feeble steps shall stay,*
> *Nor suffer thee to slide:*

Lean on thy Redeemer's breast;
He thy quiet spirit keeps;
Rest in him, securely rest;
Thy watchman never sleeps.

Neither sin, nor earth, nor hell
Thy Keeper can surprise;
Careless slumbers cannot steal
On his all-seeing eyes;
He is Israel's sure defence;
Israel all his care shall prove,
Kept by watchful providence,
And ever-waking love.

See the Lord, thy Keeper, stand
Omnipotently near!
Lo! he holds thee by thy hand
And banishes thy fear;
Shadows with his wings thy head;
Guards from all impending harms:
Round thee and beneath are spread
The everlasting arms.

Christ shall bless thy going out,
Shall bless thy coming in;
Kindly compass thee about,
Till thou art saved from sin;
Like thy spotless Master, thou,
Filled with wisdom, love, and power,
Holy, pure, and perfect, now,
Henceforth, and evermore.[1]

Biddy recalled the military funeral, at which one hundred soldiers had marched along with the gun carriage

that carried the coffin. "So many loved him," she sighed softly.

Her mind went back to another of Oswald's favorite hymns. She quickly found it and let the words lift her soul to God. In the quiet, alone with God, she felt his presence.

> *O Love that will not let me go,*
> *I rest my weary soul in Thee;*
> *I give Thee back the life I owe,*
> *That in Thine ocean depths its flow*
> *May richer, fuller be.*
>
> *O Light that foll'west all my way,*
> *I yield my flickering torch to Thee;*
> *My heart restores its borrowed ray,*
> *That in Thy sunshine's blaze its day*
> *May brighter, fairer be.*
>
> *O Joy that seekest me through pain,*
> *I cannot close my heart to Thee;*
> *I trace the rainbow through the rain,*
> *And feel the promise is not vain*
> *That morn shall tearless be.*
>
> *O Cross that liftest up my head,*
> *I dare not ask to fly from Thee;*
> *I lay in dust life's glory dead,*
> *And from the ground there blossoms red*
> *Life that shall endless be.*[2]

Biddy knew that George Matheson, the hymn's writer, was born with poor vision and that by seventeen, he was nearly blind.

Her thoughts returned to her own childhood. Her

constant ill health had forced her to miss most of the required formal education and had seriously impaired her hearing. Her sisters had helped her with her education at home.

Biddy realized that Matheson had memorized Scripture so proficiently that those who heard him speak did not know that he was blind. Biddy had learned to read lips so well that no one seemed to notice she could not hear them speaking.

"So he was blind, and I am almost deaf. We had something in common." She chuckled softly to herself. She felt her sense of humor beginning to return.

"'I trace the rainbow through the rain.'" She repeated the phrase aloud. For a moment, Biddy could almost see a soft, misty sky graced by the glorious colors of a distant rainbow.

"Not that it rains much here," she said to the rough-hewn walls as she recalled her present position: a widow with a small child, alone in the blowing sands and heat of Egypt. Just outside the door of the devotional hut stretched a vast expanse of unknowns. But the time with God had refreshed her body and restored her spirit.

Even in the desert Biddy Chambers always enjoyed an organized household. As she tidied her material at the reading table, carefully arranging notes and papers in orderly stacks, she came across a note referring to Hebrews 11:8: "He went out, not knowing where he was going." Again she remembered her husband, but somehow the pain wasn't quite so bad.

Oswald had spoken a great deal about faith, the kind of confidence in God that Abraham had shown when God called him to leave home and go to another land. Abraham hadn't questioned God. He might not have known what God was going to do, but he did know God. The key then—and now—Oswald had taught, was "to know God."

Oswald had said, "Each morning you wake it is to be a 'going out,' building confidence on God." The key word was *obedience.* Oswald's entire life was one of obedience to God.

Biddy's duty now was to continue the same quiet confidence and reliance on God.

"I will go out, trust, and obey you because I love you," she whispered to her heavenly Father. She stood, wiped her tears, straightened her long skirts, and prepared to face Egypt, World War I, hundreds of hungry soldiers, and others at the Y.M.C.A. camp where Oswald had been the chaplain to the troops at Zeitoun.

And there was four-year-old Kathleen, her daddy's "scallyway," to think of. Biddy turned her eyes away from fear and focused them on Jesus Christ the Lord.

Oswald had always said that "the Cross of God forever altered time and eternity." When a seeking soul sometimes challenged that idea, Oswald would reply, "Just because you don't believe it doesn't mean it isn't so."

They need me to be strong, Biddy decided.

The men at the Y.M.C.A. camp at Zeitoun, the volunteers, and those still praying for the work in Egypt couldn't understand why a loving God would allow the great teacher Oswald to be taken at a time when he was needed most.

Biddy, however, didn't question God's timing. She knew that to seek his face was to find the way through.

And Kathleen understood. She would put her little hand on Biddy's arm and say, "Daddy is with God. And he is quite near us now."

The heat was dreadful, the flies obnoxious, the sands intimidating, and the schedule of daily activities, including taking over Oswald's teaching, seemed like a mountain without a top. But like any other good mountain climber, Biddy knew that a climber reaches the top step by step and that proper preparation was the key to reaching the summit. Hadn't Moses climbed a mountain?

Egypt, not Biddy's home country of England, was where she was planted, and in Egypt she would bloom.

"First," she decided, "I must plan the evening meal. There are soldiers to feed. I wonder how many this time?" She knew the number of hungry stomachs could sometimes be as high as several hundred, but she still used tablecloths and proper table settings, complete with flowers in the center.

"I will go out, trust, and obey you because I love you," Biddy whispered to her heavenly Father.

"Mama? Can I ride my donkey?" Kathleen scurried into the devotional hut, looking for Biddy.

"You may, if you can," Biddy replied easily.

"Mama, are you happy again now?" Kathleen tugged at her skirts and searched her mother's face for traces of tears.

"I'm fine now," Biddy responded. "Where is your donkey?"

Kathleen skipped around the writing table.

"Is Daddy with Jesus in heaven now?" Kathleen's sad eyes searched her mother's expression.

"Yes," Biddy replied with a genuine smile.

"Isn't it lovely that Daddy is with Jesus?" Her little voice chirped comfort.

"Yes, yes. Daddy is with God." Biddy hugged her daughter close to her. "Go ahead and ride your donkey, but be certain to get help getting on and off of it."

"I will, Mama!" And Biddy's little one scampered off to find the donkey purchased for her by an Australian soldier.

As Biddy prepared for dinner, she never doubted God's provision. She simply geared up. Somehow there was always enough food to go around.

More important, however, was the spiritual food she was now to offer in addition to the evening meal. Occasionally Oswald had invited her to present the morning service. He had praised her highly for the "lift" she gave the men. "I have God's Word," she said to herself. "I will keep to that tonight."

Biddy's calm throughout the day set the tone for the camp. Eager hands reached out to help her with the daily chores, while loving hearts and earnest prayers lifted her to the throne of grace.

She realized that the men who listened that evening would return to the battle line the next morning. They would carry their Bibles, and they would face the possibility of serious injury or death at dawn.

"God provides," Biddy said, opening a Bible. She found, "Whoso looketh into the perfect law of liberty, and continueth therein, he being not a forgetful hearer, but a doer of the work, this man shall be blessed in his deed" (James 1:25, KJV).

Biddy remembered that Oswald believed in "doing" rather than in simply talking about what might be done.

He disciplined himself to pick himself up and go. He would want Biddy to do the same.

Without another thought, she plunged ahead. She knew without a doubt that the key to bearing fruit was to obey God's Word.

She didn't have much time to prepare. Constant interruptions did not deter her while she focused on the message to the men. She did not quit. With eyes looking steadily toward Jesus, her fingers quickly jotted notes.

She would tell the men that God loved them. She would also tell them that God was waiting for them to love him. It was simple. And it lifted her own heart. She based the talk on the book of Hosea, where God speaks plainly about his relationship to humankind: "I desired mercy, and not sacrifice; and the knowledge of God more than burnt offerings" (Hosea 6:6, KJV).

It seemed like no time at all before she was prepared. "Yes," she said quietly, "this will do nicely."

Biddy Chambers stood, patted her hair in place, smoothed the wrinkles from her skirts, brushed the dust off her shoes, picked up her materials, and headed toward the waiting soldiers.

"Only two minutes late," she noted with a smile.

"We all, with open face beholding as in a glass the glory of the Lord, are changed into the same image from glory to glory, even as by the Spirit of the Lord" (2 Corinthians 3:18, KJV).

The Word spoke. Biddy Chambers obeyed, and she reflected God's love.

FOUR

$\mathscr{S}$tream

LONDON/BRITISH COLUMBIA
1994

> *[Jesus said,] "By this all will know that you are My*
> *disciples, if you have love for one another."* JOHN 13:35

When Miss Kathleen Chambers in England answered my
telephone call that sunny September day in 1994, I stood
rooted to the spot. As I carefully replaced the receiver after
our conversation, I wondered, *Can a long-distance conversa-*
tion be considered the same as standing on holy ground?

Probably not, I reasoned. But I knew that greatness had
crossed my path.

Feeling overwhelmed, I decided I needed chocolate.
Hopping into my automobile, I rationalized all the way to
the local grocery store. *After all, dark chocolate is supposed*
to be good for one, isn't it? Because it contains antisomethings
that combat future illness. Anyway, that's what I heard on the
news today.

As I entered the store, I pushed aside my guilty feelings about how I was going to destroy my faltering girlish figure, ruin my life with the fat and caffeine in chocolate, and prevent myself from sleeping for a week, and hurriedly pushed a cart down the candy aisle.

"Oh, no, there isn't any," I commented to the older woman standing by the jelly beans.

"Isn't any what?"

"Chocolate."

"What kind are you looking for?" Her sweet smile lit up her twinkly blue eyes.

I guessed her to be somewhere in her seventies, but I was certain she never ate chocolate. Only fruits and vegetables. After all, she sported a sharp shape and lovely complexion.

"Oh," I mumbled, "the dark kind."

Instead of getting the look of disapproval I expected, I saw the woman's countenance brighten.

"Ah, my favorite too," she replied, reaching under some misplaced jelly beans. "They're all right here. How many would you like?"

"I'm still thinking," I replied, trying hard to look nonplussed.

By the time I exited the friendly market, I had learned the woman was ninety years old, did eat chocolate, did not always get the required five-to-seven fruits and veggies every day—and ate butter!

It turned out that she had also read *My Utmost for His Highest* but didn't know that Oswald and Biddy Chambers had a daughter named Kathleen, let alone that *B. C.* in the preface stood for *Biddy Chambers*. She advised me to continue my search for information.

"This is a story that needs to be told," she had counseled.

In my heart, I knew she was right. Consequently, when I returned home, I forgot all about the chocolate I had purchased and went straight to my typewriter, where I tapped out, "Choose circumstances carefully. Your choices carry you like a stick floating on the stream of life. Once afloat, the stick has no choice but to be propelled toward the river's destination. Unless it is plucked out, it is one with the water's end."

Biddy Chambers had made her choice to follow Jesus at any cost. She also loved her husband and supported his choice to love Jesus above all else. In all things, Biddy allowed Jesus Christ to shine for all men to see. And Kathleen, the dear person I was coming to know, chose to live a life of service and sacrifice too.

"The interesting thing to me," I whispered quietly, still at the typewriter, "is that not one of them intended to be known. Their only goal was to know Jesus. It's all about choices."

Early the next morning, England time (the middle of the night for me), I telephoned Kathleen Chambers again.

We agreed to write letters to each other, and I was astounded to discover that she had read my books. "How did you know about my books?" I queried.

"We read in England, too, you know. We even have television." Her tone was kind, and her wit quick.

And so, the friendship across the ocean, and across the sands of time, began. As we shared information about the practical realities of her everyday life and mine, I realized then, and have not forgotten, that God's love flows through his children. All we have to do is to love him and obey him. It has been the same since the beginning. Through

Kathleen's eyes, I was enabled to begin to see the spectacular stream of God's love and "an endless river of righteous living" (Amos 5:24, NLT) flowing throughout time.

About a week later, Kathleen said, "By the way, I liked your books—"

"Thank you," I interrupted.

"—because you have a great sense of humor," she finished.

"I don't know why people laugh," I replied quickly. "I cry when I write them."

"Cry? Why?" Kathleen seemed to care about people in a special way.

"Because it is serious stuff!"

Dead silence. She was listening.

"You see," I began, "that is why I would like to write a book about your mother, so that women today can see that God carries each and every generation, and that Jesus Christ liberated women and set them free, and that there is no other way to really gain the peace that only he can give. It cannot be attained by achievement; no matter how great—"

For once Kathleen broke in. "That is why I want you to write my mother's story."

"Really?"

"Yes. I like your sense of humor. She said not to ever trust a Christian without a sense of humor."

I greatly appreciated Kathleen's trust, so I launched into my vision of her mother's story. "The biography of your mother will be a portrait—not a photograph—of her life. The focus will be God. The idea is to lift Jesus higher in the hearts of those who read the book and to allow them to love Biddy Chambers as I already do. *Searching for Mrs. Oswald*

Chambers will show what God did for Oswald's wife out of his love for her. I believe she lived her life in response to the love of God and that her life's work was her gift of love to him."

"And now, you really must hang up," Kathleen said. "This must be very expensive for you." She promised to write soon.

I followed her suggestion.

Her first letter was dated October 5, 1994. Some of what she wrote follows:

> *Dear Marsha Drake [my real name, not my pen name],*
> *It was such a real pleasure to talk to you the other day—I am so glad you persevered until you got me. I liked what you said about my mother, and your "woman's outlook" sounded just right to me.*
>
> *Please forgive my atrocious writing. I have had arthritis since I was 13 years old, mainly in my back but I drive and shop and . . . walk to hospital & church. I look after my old house and dog. My mother and I had a really good relationship. We always had an open house with unlocked and open doors & everyone was welcome specially children & animals. My mother had an infectious laugh. She was practically stone deaf in one ear.*
>
> *She had a hearing aid which was very unsatisfactory because it accentuated every small sound. She got very tired as a result and could catnap for 5 minutes & wake up completely refreshed. All the typing and letter writing was done with constant interruptions of shopping, cooking, & cups of tea.*
>
> *I always wanted to nurse & I did my training at one of London's big hospitals & then I nursed . . . in the*

*overcrowded poverty stricken districts in London & brought
many of the kids back home including their . . .*

I was never able to figure out what she brought home. I
always wanted to ask her but never had the opportunity.
Kathleen was very courageous; therefore, it could have been
anything. The words looked like *fleas & bugs!!* And the excla-
mation points were hers.

Her letter concluded,

> *I am going to take pity on you and stop writing or I'll
> weary you.*
> *I am delighted to get to know you.*
>
> *With love,*
> *Kathleen*

I called her at least once a week, and we corresponded
by mail. Following is part of my letter to her written
October 21, 1994:

> *Dear Kathleen,*
> *I so enjoyed talking with you on the phone this
> morning! Wish it weren't so expensive. I would call more
> often.*
> *You mentioned arthritis. Let's get one thing clear right
> now—I cannot spell—I'm just a bit dyslexic, just great for
> someone who taught English and so forth. I always tell my
> students not to be afraid to tell me if I've spelled something
> wrong. And I can understand arthritis and back trouble
> because I injured my back in my early twenties, and I have
> a double curved spine and arthritis.*

What my question is—how did you manage to nurse with a bad back? Didn't you have to do a lot of lifting?

What kind of dog do you have? I have one too, named Cookie. He's a toy poodle and Pomeranian cross—very tiny—but he has the heart of a sheep dog, in that he directs sheep, mainly me. Dogs are great!

As a matter of fact, he is sitting beside me "talking" right now about the game of fetch-and-carry he'd like to play with his toy hamburger. The game is, he throws it and I retrieve it.

Kathleen broke in, "That is why I want you to write my mother's story. I like your sense of humor. My mother said not to ever trust a Christian without a sense of humor."

Thanks for telling me about you and your mother. I think I will learn about a great many things from you while writing a book. I so appreciate your outlook on Christianity and life. It is real.

The sun is shining brightly today after several days of cold rain. I like the rain though. Thank you so much for being you.

My best love,
Marsha

During our next transatlantic phone call, we agreed that I would begin historical research and that we could try using a tape recorder in order to keep her from having to write letters.

She also volunteered to see what else she could find to send to me.

I waited exactly twenty-four hours before I called her again. "Kathleen?"

"Yes."

I knew she knew it was me, but I said, "It's me, Marsha."

"Yes."

"Were you around when your mother was writing?"

"The books?"

"I mean, did you help her?"

"Oh," Kathleen chuckled. "Yes, I shoveled coal into the stove. We had to keep warm, you know, Ducks."

"Oh." My voice registered my disappointment.

"Really, I was a small child during most of the writing of the books. But I have friends who knew my mother. Would you like me to get in touch with them?"

"Oh, yes!" I clapped my hands together in glee. "And may I write to them?"

"Yes, you may."

I loved her crisp English accent with words delivered in well-modulated tones.

"And can I send them a list of questions to answer about your mother?"

"You may, if you can." Kathleen often corrected my sloppy use of the English language.

"Okay," I laughed. "I'll make up a list of questions and mail them to you today so that you can think about them."

I hung up the telephone, and I went to work right away. This is some of what I wrote and sent to Kathleen via airmail that same day:

Biddy Chambers

QUESTIONS: Please *type* your answers or *print* them clearly on a separate sheet of paper. Thank you.

What was your relationship to Mrs. Chambers? By what name did you call her: Biddy, or Mrs. Chambers, or _____?

Please complete the following sentence (expand your answer to fit the situation): When I first met B. C., my first impression was _____.

Did you know Oswald first? How long did you know him?

If you knew Biddy Chambers's thoughts on prayer, please write all you know about her prayer life. Did she pray with you?

Can you remember the *year* you met Biddy Chambers?

In your opinion, did Biddy ever give way to despair?

Please describe Biddy Chambers [physically] as you remember seeing her.

What, would you say, was her strongest character trait?

Did B. C. ever do any devotional writing of her own, or did she spend all of her time writing Oswald Chambers's teachings?

While walking to the post office, I thought about some of the things Kathleen had told me about her mother.

"Kathleen, did your mother ever talk to you about when your father died—that he was so young, and it was so unexpected?"

"Yes. My mother told me that she had thought it was not a sickness unto death, so she was puzzled. She wondered what it meant. After all, he went into hospital for a simple appendectomy, and he died a few days later from complications. She often wondered about that."

"But she never doubted God? I mean, sometimes I hear people say that they are mad at God."

"No, Marsha. She never doubted God. In fact, my father's death meant life in Christ to thousands. The books were never promoted by my mother. She simply obeyed God, and the books came to be."

Arriving at the front of my house, I realized the importance of simply obeying God. But I knew it wasn't easy. For Mrs. Oswald Chambers, it had cost a great deal. But B. C. had obeyed God out of her love for him.

Humbled by her example, I paused at the front door before I turned the key.

"Hello? Anybody home?" The silence of an empty house gave me peace. Grabbing my Bible, I went straight to my rocking chair, settled in, and read the words of Jesus in Matthew 7:7-11:

> Keep on asking, and you will receive what you ask for. Keep on seeking, and you will find. Keep on knocking, and the door will be opened to you. For everyone who asks, receives. Everyone who seeks, finds. And to everyone who knocks, the door will be opened.
>
> You parents—if your children ask for a loaf of bread, do you give them a stone instead? Or if they ask for a fish, do you give them a snake? Of course not! So if you sinful people know how to give good gifts to your

children, how much more will your heavenly Father give good gifts to those who ask him. (NLT)

Gazing out the window at a blue sky studded with fluffy clouds, I whispered, "Please, God, enable me to obey you out of love too."

As I quietly rocked back and forth, I realized a great truth. The mighty stream that I was following flowed from heaven in the beginning. It was still flowing in modern times. After all, the apostle Paul said, "You should imitate me, just as I imitate Christ" (1 Corinthians 11:1, NLT).

Following the stream would take me deep into the woods of the unknown. What would I discover about this godly woman, Mrs. Oswald Chambers? The words of Jesus spoke to my heart: *Keep on asking, and you will receive what you ask for.*

Like a child blowing out candles on a birthday cake, I closed my eyes in happy expectation. Instead of making a wish, however, I asked God for a long list of things that I knew in my heart he would provide. That much I had already learned from Kathleen.

A bright future full of delightful discovery beckoned.

FIVE

𝒯ruda

LONDON/BRITISH COLUMBIA
1994

> *No one can lay any foundation other than the one we*
> *already have—Jesus Christ.* 1 CORINTHIANS 3:11, NLT

Her given name was Gertrude Hobbs.

I didn't even know what year she was born. It could have
been 1883 or 1884. Her birthday was always celebrated on
July 13. I was certain, however, that her place of birth was
Eltham, England.

I knew that because in the year of our Lord 1994, my
newfound friend, Miss Kathleen Chambers, began answer-
ing my questions about her mother during our transatlantic
telephone conversations.

I also spent a great deal of time trying to find information on my own. I discovered through old church records
in Eltham, England, that Gertrude Hobbs had had an older
brother and sister.

Although much of my interest had been sparked by my curiosity about B. C., I was also captivated by the description of the virtuous woman outlined in Proverbs 31. As a woman living in the modern world, I was particularly interested in this question: Can a woman today live like that virtuous woman? Has anyone ever really done that? I knew about Queen Esther, in the Old Testament, and others, but what about today? I was spending a lot of time reading Proverbs and trying to absorb the great wisdom outlined there in order to "know wisdom and instruction, to perceive the words of understanding" (Proverbs 1:2).

When I discovered that Miss Gertrude Hobbs had been born into a family of Bible-believing Christians, I knew she would have received all the best advice God had to offer because her family read and adhered to the teaching of the Bible: "The fear of the LORD is the beginning of knowledge, but fools despise wisdom and instruction" (Proverbs 1:7).

All Gertrude would have to do one day was to make the faith of her fathers her very own. I was convinced of the truth of God's Word, which says, "Train up a child in the way he should go [and in keeping with his individual gift or bent], and when he is old he will not depart from it" (Proverbs 22:6, AMP).

Since Gertrude would have received proper training and a knowledge of God's Word, she would have been steeped in the wisdom given by the Lord.

That fact established, I moved on to other things.

What kind of world was baby Gertrude born into? What would be expected of a girl living in the nineteenth century?

Of course, that world did not contain our modern conveniences. I found an interesting perspective on how women's lives have changed when I read an 1884 guide on how to prepare flour from wheat:

1. Grind the wheat between two horizontal stones, the upper one revolving and convex, the lower one stationary and concave.
2. Divide the result into bran, coarse flour, and fine flour.
3. Discard the bran as "utterly useless for human food."
4. The coarse flour contains little gluten and is inferior.
5. The fine flour, heated by grinding, must be cooled and dried or it will spoil rapidly.
6. Use the fine flour to make breads, cakes, or pastry.[1]

So much for toast first thing in the morning!

In the Victorian era (so called because it was the time when Queen Victoria reigned), there were no washing machines, microwaves, computers, or remote light switches, but one of the biggest differences between that era and our own was the place of women in society.

There were perceptive women of independent, original thought, but for the huge majority, life was easier if they accepted that a woman's place was in the home.

The accepted reasoning of the time was that the career for women was marriage. To get ready for courtship and marriage, a girl was groomed like a racehorse. In addition to being able to sing, play an instrument, and speak a little French or Italian, young Victorian gentlewomen were to be innocent, virtuous, dutiful, and ignorant of intellectual opinion.

Whether married or single, Victorian women were seen as weak and helpless, fragile, delicate flowers incapable of making decisions beyond selecting the day's menu. If she was married, her primary responsibility was to bear a large family, ensure that her children were taught moral values, and see to it that the home was a place of comfort for her husband and family, a sanctuary from the stresses of industrial Britain. Her husband assumed that his house would run smoothly so he could get on with making money.

Gertrude Hobbs was born into a world where a married woman could not even own property. Her inheritance from her family became her husband's property once she was married. If a wife separated from her husband, even for legitimate reasons, she had no rights of access to see her children. A divorced woman had no chance of acceptance in society again.

So much for the life of a single mother. "If Gertrude had any idea of what life would hold for her, she might have changed her mind and not been born," I muttered, shuffling through more research notes. "Not that she could have chosen, of course!" I smiled as I stacked the papers into orderly piles.

My research was giving me a headache. *It's a good thing I have Kathleen to talk to,* I told myself. Then I went for a much-needed walk to relieve some tension.

When I got back to my research, I found that in Gertrude's day a wealthy wife was supposed to spend her time reading, sewing, receiving guests, visiting other women, writing letters, seeing to the servants, and dressing appropriately for her role as her husband's social representative. That didn't seem so bad.

But for the poor of Britain, things were quite different. Fifth-hand clothes were the norm. Servants ate the pickings that were left over in the households where they served. The average mill worker could afford only the most inferior food: rancid bacon, tired vegetables, green potatoes, stringy meat, tainted bread, porridge, cheese, and herrings or kippers.

I thought young Gertrude Hobbs might have picked a man able to provide financially for her. From what I understood, making money was not the first priority for Oswald Chambers. He believed what the Bible said, which was to seek God's Kingdom first and let God take care of the particulars. At one point he gave away his last shilling to a man walking on the street!

Kathleen Chambers, Gertrude and Oswald's daughter, opened the door to possibilities of really learning to know God, and I was always excited and looking forward to our next conversation or to the next letter from her, all the way from England.

I thought young Gertrude Hobbs might have picked a man able to provide financially for her. From what I understood, making money was not the first priority for Oswald Chambers. At one point he gave away his last shilling to a man walking on the street!

As time went on, I got used to getting up at about three in the morning in order to speak to Kathleen in the "real" morning, England time.

Since I was calling all the way to England, I had expected Kathleen to have trouble hearing me, so I raised the volume of my voice to "loud and clear."

"Can you hear me?" I had also figured Kathleen must be

in her early eighties, and I didn't want her to have to strain to listen.

"Yes. You don't need to shout."

So much for my polite effort. I had probably given her a headache, but I pushed on anyway. "Sorry if I broke your eardrum. You sound like you're right next door." I was still amazed at how close she sounded.

"Yes. We've had telephones here for a long time now." She paused. Dead silence.

"I've been wondering what would happen if somebody really tried to live like the woman outlined in Proverbs 31, because women today are really moving forward in business and politics and the world in general. So how does that relate to what I've been reading in the Bible?"

I didn't expect an answer. Miss Chambers was an excellent listener. Later, I would discover how she had honed her skills: She was her mother's daughter. She taught by example.

"Anyway, Miss Chambers—I mean, Kathleen—when I was researching godly women in the Bible, I discovered that the virtuous wife in Proverbs seemed to be a super-human lady of extraordinary talents. She got up before dawn (no small feat since she also worked far into the night), she procured wool and flax and managed to spin it (I've never even seen a spinning wheel except in a museum), and she made the clothes for her entire household."

I paused. "Are you still there?"

"Yes."

"Oh, good! Well, then, let's not forget the fact that this virtuous woman was also a businesswoman. She had servant girls, and she planned their day's work at whatever time the sun came up."

I paused for air. "Are you still there, Kathleen?"

"Yes."

"Can you stand a little more?"

"Yes. This is interesting."

"Well, anyway, this incredible woman was married to an important man who sat in council chambers, probably making important decisions for the local townsfolk, or the nation, or possibly the world, and I'm trying to see if there is another woman anywhere in the world who lives like that."

"Go on."

"Okay. I'll summarize."

At that point, Kathleen contributed a delightfully hearty chuckle to our conversation.

Encouraged, I continued. "I'll just read my list. Here's what I discovered about the woman in Proverbs 31:

- She has the trust of her husband.
- She satisfies her husband (one Bible version added the word *richly*).
- She helps her husband her entire life.
- She never thwarts her mate.
- She buys wool and flax and processes it into fabric.
- She buys food from all over the world.
- She goes to the ship ports herself to see the merchandise.
- She's up before dawn and prepares breakfast— for everyone in the house.
- She plans the day for her servants.
- She inspects some acreage and buys it.
- She plants a vineyard.
- She is tireless.
- She has strong arms (in other words, she's physically fit).

- She works for the poor in her community.
- In her spare time, she sews for the needy.
- She makes her own clothes.
- (And my personal belief is that her calories self-destruct. I mean, in those days women probably didn't worry about their weight the way we do today.)"

All the while I was reading my list to Kathleen, I kept thinking, *I am speaking to the daughter of one of the great theologians of our time, and she lets me call her by her first name!*

Since I was brought up in the United States a very long time ago, I was trained in proper manners and polite decorum. Teachers, ministers, doctors, and especially the president expected to be addressed properly. Even a difference in age required a "Mrs." or "Sir" or "Yes, ma'am." Therefore, since Kathleen sported senior status, I was surprised she gave me permission to address her by her first name.

Kathleen, how is it that you don't know the exact year your mother was born? Actually, I wanted to ask that, but I decided it would have sounded impertinent. Instead I asked, "Your mother was born in Eltham, England? I'm not too good at geography. Can you give me an idea of where that is, exactly?"

I waited for her to answer. She didn't.

"I'm serious," I persisted. "I found London, England, on the map, but I can't find Eltham. Does it still exist?"

The sound of her amusement traveled through the phone lines.

"You laughed," I commented. "That's nice!"

"My mother had an infectious chuckle," she offered. "My mother and my father were very much against pretense of any kind. Jesus expressed amusement, didn't he?"

To Kathleen, biblical truths were part of everyday activity.

I hung on her every word as she continued.

She began to expound. Kathleen's mother, Gertrude Hobbs, was born into a world of hard work. Nothing was easy at the end of the nineteenth century. Before the invention of washing machines, the heavy clothes were soaked in washtubs and rubbed over corrugated washboards. Doing laundry was back-breaking work.

For Gertrude's mother, keeping the children clothed and fed must have taken most of the day.

Even the little things we now take for granted to make life easier, ball-point pens, for example, were not available. About the time Gertrude was born, the first practical fountain pen containing its own ink reservoir was patented in America. So much for making grocery lists. And certainly, no daily planners were available.

The end of the nineteenth century saw the invention of the lightbulb, but more important, it saw the birth of a light bearer for Jesus Christ. Could anyone have realized how great the impact of the life of one little girl would be on the entire world?

The end of the nineteenth century saw the invention of the lightbulb, but more important, it saw the birth of a light bearer for Jesus Christ. Could anyone have realized how great the impact of the life of one little girl would be on the entire world?

When I asked Kathleen to describe her mother to me, she responded, "I loved her all my life." In today's world, many daughters might respond differently. Kathleen loved her mother unconditionally. And she imitated her mother's behavior by showering the love of Christ on all with whom she came in contact. I was no exception.

Kathleen lived out her faith in God and his Word, which told her to "live a life filled with love, following the example of Christ. He loved us and offered himself as a sacrifice for us, a pleasing aroma to God" (Ephesians 5:2, NLT).

In my notes I wrote, "Love leads the way."

At one time, Kathleen had been a nurse and worked in the slums of England. I reasoned that because she was probably used to dealing with difficult patients, she had taken my first phone call in stride. On the other hand, maybe it was because she was incredibly kind. Kathleen took in stray cats, dogs, students, and even children. She followed in the footsteps of her mother, whose heart and home were a haven to anyone who needed her help. Although Kathleen had no children of her own, she had strong maternal instincts, which drew me to her because I had lost my mother at a relatively early age. When I was talking to the daughter of Oswald Chambers, I felt as if it were Christmas morning and I had found my favorite gift under the tree. My delight in finding Kathleen was enormous.

As Kathleen Chambers reminisced, she revealed a role model for modern Christian women. I had struck gold. Her mother, the "B. C." at the beginning of *My Utmost for His Highest,* was incredible. Could her example light the way for the women of today, who juggle marriage, children, career, separation, loss, fatigue, illness, joy, and disappointment?

A journey into the Chambers legacy took me from fiction to reality.

Amazing truths began to unfold as Kathleen extended a hand of friendship to a struggling pilgrim.

Just as she learned early in life by watching her parents' example, she generously handed Christ's love to me. Kathleen's mother had followed Christ. So did Kathleen.

"Kathleen, may we talk again?"

"Yes," she responded warmly.

"And will you tell me about your mother's childhood?"

"Yes. She was called Truda."

$\mathscr{P}$ath

LONDON
Early 1900s

> *Do all things without complaining and disputing,*
> *that you may become blameless and harmless,*
> *children of God without fault in the midst of a*
> *crooked and perverse generation, among whom you*
> *shine as lights in the world.* PHILIPPIANS 2:14-15

When Kathleen entered my life, she put me on a path leading ever upward. But not with the magnanimity of personal
prominence. Kathleen, like her mother, Gertrude Hobbs
Chambers, imparted the touch of the One who has changed
human lives for two thousand years, "for the Kingdom of
God is not just a lot of talk; it is living by God's power"
(1 Corinthians 4:20, NLT).

Because of the Chambers legacy, the teachings of Jesus,
who walked the hillsides and sat with the unacceptable and
unloved, would take deeper root in my spirit.

"How about just telling me whatever you like about your mother's childhood? For example, why was she called Truda?"

"She was also called Gertie."

"Just a nickname, then?" I was getting nowhere fast. "Kathleen, what would you think if I let you tell all of this to me your way?"

"Good idea, Ducks," she quickly answered. "I will write it to you in a letter and hope you can read my awful handwriting." Her laughter bubbled like a gentle brook on a warm summer's day.

That decided, we terminated the connection.

In a few days, true to her promise, Kathleen wrote to me about her mother, Gertrude Hobbs, and about her maternal grandmother, and I was able to read most of it! Kathleen was a great correspondent and had inherited the gift of scintillating syntax from her parents.

Dear Marsha,

I'll try to keep my writing large & legible, Ducks.

My grandmother, Mrs. Hobbs, lived in Eltham, South East London, & she had three children, 2 daughters & a son. My grandfather died when my mother was in her teens. My mother had bronchitis every year while she was in school & lost a lot of schooling. She left school, anyway, when she was about fourteen, & learnt Pitman' shorthand by a correspondence course, & my grandmother & aunt read to her to get up her speed till eventually she had a speed of 275 words a minute. She was very ambitious & wanted to become secretary to the prime minister!

The first job she had was as secretary to General Sir

William Norris . . . [I never could figure out from her handwriting if it was Norris or Morris, and I never had a chance to ask her] *at Woolwich Arsenal.*

Once I discovered that Woolwich Arsenal was located in Kent, England, I decided to do some research to find out more about where Gertrude Hobbs worked on her first job. Since most people speak at a rate of one hundred eighty to two hundred words per minute, Truda's speed and accuracy in taking shorthand were outstanding.

She must have been a greatly valued employee, I reasoned, while reading Kathleen's letter. In order to understand more about Truda's first job as a secretary, I forged ahead, digging for details.

My investigation about the Woolwich Arsenal revealed the following:

The Royal Arsenal, Woolwich, manufactured big guns, shells and other munitions for the army and navy. The name the Royal Arsenal was awarded in 1805.

By the First World War, the site covered two square miles and over 80,000 were employed there in the manufacture of munitions.

The iron-framed Armstrong Gun Factory (1856) still stands and is used as a British Library store. Nearby were former Shrinking Pits, cast-iron lined well shafts filled with oil into which red hot gun barrels were plunged to shrink them out of their liners.[1]

Photos reveal that the sheer size of the complex intimidates visitors even today. Huge buildings, drafty high windows, circular metal stairwells, brick and stone walls, and humming activity greeted young Truda, by then in her teens, when she arrived for work.

To me, the fact that she could even make it up those narrow stairs while wearing high-button shoes was nothing short of a miracle, not to mention the task of navigating the rough cement floors in long skirts. And I had read somewhere that in those days, women often fainted for lack of air because of the constricting corsets they wore to create the fashionable hourglass figures. Truda, however, valiantly forged ahead.

I took a break for a glass of water, then returned to my study.

I could not believe what I had uncovered. Truda worked for a gun factory! Later, during one of our long-distance, transatlantic phone conversations, Kathleen told me that her mother "worked there for some time."

Truda's next job was quite different. As a secretary for a barrister (an attorney) in Lincoln's Inn Fields, the center of London's law world, she typed legal briefs, which had to be immaculate, "no alterations *ever,* very exacting," Kathleen had written.

That took me back to the first job I had as a typist one summer when I was sixteen. Since I had barely made it through typing class in high school, I was worried when the Lady in Charge sat me in front of a manual typewriter, handed me a pile of legal-looking paperwork, and said, "Have these done by noon today."

I began to type. After a couple of words, I made a mistake. Embarrassed, I glanced around to see if any of the other typists madly turning out perfect papers on their electric typewriters had noticed. They hadn't.

"So far, so good," I muttered.

Since I could use nothing—not erasers, not white correction liquid—to fix mistakes, I blanched in embarrassment when I felt my fingers go completely in the wrong direction. Glancing at the typed copy, I confirmed the worst. Not one, but *five* mistakes in the first three words, which included the date and the name of the document.

Then I managed to type one word correctly—while looking at the keys (a real no-no in typing class).

Realizing that I was in serious trouble, I threw that ruined document into the trash. It was nine o'clock in the morning.

By ten o'clock, the wastebasket was full, and I was scared. *What if I can't do it?*

The voice of calm replied, *Try, and you will succeed.*

By eleven-thirty, I was sailing along, typing as carefully as I could. I no longer paid any attention to the other secretaries. I no longer listened for their intimidating, accurate *tap-tap-tapping* as they produced flawless legal papers.

I knew for certain that *this* time I had made no mistakes, and I was coming to the end of the document I was supposed to type.

I could taste success.

Then I glanced up at the wall clock to see how close I was to high noon, and my eyes fell on the typewriter. I was typing on the empty typewriter roller.

In my effort to be accurate and not to peek at my typing, I failed to notice that the paper had slipped right out of the machine and fallen to the floor behind my typing station.

Just then, I heard a cathedral clock somewhere in the distance chime twelve times.

Suddenly, from out of nowhere, the Lady in Charge, who had assigned my task at nine o'clock in the morning, appeared at my left elbow. "Maybe this isn't for you," she gently suggested.

I hung my head in shame. "Guess not," I replied, trying not to cry.

The attorney's office was on the forty-first floor of a prestigious building in a very large city. Too humiliated to take the elevator, I walked down forty-one flights of stairs to the busy street.

When I arrived home, I emptied my pockets and purse of all the extra paper I'd stuffed into them after the trash can was too full to hold any more typing rejects.

I never told my mother. But during our next phone call, I did tell Kathleen. And Kathleen listened, and she cared.

She offered the touch of the One who makes guilt go away and produces victory instead. The more we spoke, the more I realized that Kathleen's love healed the pain of that particular mortifying failure, and I felt the touch of Jesus on my soul.

Truda Hobbs had typed for all of us who never quite made it, and as Kathleen would say, "I was happy about that."

As I listened to Kathleen's wisdom born of faith and experience, peace invaded my soul, and I felt honored to be in her company. She had a quick wit. Laughter came easily to her, and our many conversations covered normal topics such as the weather and autumn as well as my interest in her and her family.

Kathleen cherished all the children who came her way, never refusing to offer her time and interest. In doing so, she followed the path of her mother, Biddy.

Her father, Oswald, also spoke of the need to have the faith of a little child.

Kathleen told me that Jesus taught that childlike faith, not common sense or intellect, was most important to God. When the disciples had no time for the faith of small children, Jesus called to them and said, "Let the children come to me. Don't stop them! For the Kingdom of God belongs to those who are like these children. I tell you the truth, anyone who doesn't receive the Kingdom of God like a child will never enter it" (Luke 18:16-17, NLT).

Truda Hobbs had typed for all of us who never quite made it, and as Kathleen would say, "I was happy about that."

Both Kathleen and her mother, Gertrude, had the simple faith of a child, but they also had the wisdom and spiritual beauty of the woman described in Proverbs 31.

"It must be possible, through Christ Jesus, to live like that today," I whispered while closing the pile of books on my desk and gathering my notes into a somewhat neat stack.

Early the next morning, England time, I called again. "Kathleen! I'm so glad you answered the phone. I loved your letter. Thank you so much." She welcomed my enthusiasm.

After we talked, she closed the conversation by assigning a task for me to perform. "Ducks, I want you to remember to eat. Make some hard-boiled eggs and get some sleep. Jesus was very practical, you know."

"Yes, ma'am," I responded meekly.

"By the way," she continued, changing the subject, "my dog's name is Lady. And she's afraid of thunderstorms, but she and I get through them together."

In the same way that she loved God's other creatures, Kathleen loved Lady.

"Kathleen? One more thing." I didn't want to sever the connection.

"Yes?"

"Do you think God always answers prayer?"

"Yes."

"Do you have a favorite verse in the Bible?"

"Yes, Isaiah 32:17."

After hanging up the receiver, I looked up the reference and read, "Righteousness will bring peace. Yes, it will bring quietness and confidence forever" (NLT).

I printed it out and hung it on my wall, and I'm looking at it still.

Today, Kathleen Chambers is in glory with her father, Oswald, and her mother, Gertrude. She lives because Jesus Christ is the same yesterday, today, and for always.

SEVEN

*O*swald

ENGLAND
1905

> *Go therefore and make disciples of all the nations,*
> *baptizing them in the name of the Father and of*
> *the Son and of the Holy Spirit, teaching them to*
> *observe all things that I have commanded you;*
> *and lo, I am with you always, even to the end of*
> *the age.*   MATTHEW 28:19-20

In 1905, when twenty-two-year-old Gertrude Hobbs grace-fully straightened her long skirts and settled into a seat near the front of Eltham Park Baptist Church, near London, England, to hear the morning message, she was in for a surprise.

Instead of the pastor, Arthur Chambers, his brother Oswald, age thirty-one, stood before the assembled worshipers to deliver a special Sunday-morning sermon.

As Gertrude gazed steadily forward and waited to hear

Oswald speak, she noticed his lean frame and sincere countenance. More than that, she was captivated by the power of his oratory. She was ready to hear about a deeper call to follow Christ.

In a letter Kathleen explained why her mother had first attended the Baptist church in Eltham:

> My father's eldest brother was a Baptist minister in Eltham. My grandmother, on my mother's side, and her family were members of his church and they always entertained a visiting minister, and when my father came to preach (when he was in college in Scotland) he would have meals at my grandmother's house, and that's where my father met my mother, and when my mother went to the USA, it coincided with my father's visit to the USA, and my grandmother asked him to look after my mother on the voyage, which embarrassed and delighted her!!

The next morning I was on the telephone. "Kathleen, why did your mother go to the United States? I can't read that part of the letter."

With her usual patience, Kathleen helped me to decipher the writing. The letter had continued:

> Mother had a great friend, Marian, who was also a secretary (I'm named after her. My second name is Marian) and Marian applied for a job in the USA, and went to the USA and persuaded my mother to apply too, which my mother did and she went to America by sea. It took ten days and cost . . .

(I never could figure that part out, but I think it wasn't very expensive.)

They shared the same boarding house. Mother came back to England when her job finished, but Marian stayed on, got married and stayed in the USA.

It's very difficult to get any of these details in any proper order. . . .

Kathleen's letter concluded,

I do hope this wasn't too awful to read.

Much love,
Kathleen.

The story captivated me, so I began more research on my own. Who was Oswald Chambers? And what would motivate Gertrude's mother to entrust her daughter to a single man on a transatlantic voyage?

From Miles J. Stanford, Christian author (1914–1999), I learned the following:

Oswald Chambers (1874–1917) was born in Aberdeen, Scotland. He was educated in The Art School in South Kensington, the University of Edinburgh, and in theology in Dunoon Training School, where he became a tutor in philosophy. From 1906 to 1907, Oswald engaged in a round-the-world preaching tour among Methodist and Holiness groups.[1] While studying at Dunoon Training College under the leadership of the principal, Rev. Duncan MacGregor, Oswald found a closer walk with God.

Rev. MacGregor gathered young Christian men around him and taught them theology, Hebrew, and Greek. He prepared them for the ministry. It was a small school in size, but large in spiritual stature.

If a student could pay for expenses, it was expected, but if a student was unable to pay, the acceptance was the same.

Everyone worked in the college and in the garden, and students were trained to look after themselves just as would be required on a foreign mission field.

For the period that Oswald studied at Dunoon, God was shaping him as yielding clay on his wheel. Oswald learned to say with Paul, "I also count all things loss for the excellence of the knowledge of Christ Jesus my Lord" (Philippians 3:8). My mind had been reeling while I tried to figure out what had happened in the life of Oswald Chambers. But finally, the pieces of the time puzzle seemed to be coming together.

In 1905, there was a spiritual revival sweeping across Wales, and Arthur Chambers, Oswald's brother, with the blessing of his church, went to Wales to see what it was all about.

During that time, Gertrude Hobbs and her sister, Edith, had recently been baptized and joined Arthur's church in Eltham, England.

Oswald was drawn to the revival because people of dissimilar denominations and social classes were coming together. Instead of debating differences, the believers lived in harmony. The bottom line for everyone was faith in Christ. It seemed that only the Holy Spirit could have brought this about.

It was called the Holiness Movement, and it began in 1824 and lasted until about 1923. The basic concept of the Holiness Movement was to love God with all one's heart, mind, and soul, to live a life free of committing conscious or deliberate acts of sin, to observe carefully the divine ordinances of God, and to exhibit a humble and steadfast reliance on God's forgiveness and atonement. The proponents and followers of the Holiness Movement also looked for God's glory in all things and sought an increasing exercise of the love which fulfills the entire law of God.[2]

To my way of thinking, the book of Acts described this "Holiness Movement" sweeping the land, not only in Wales but around the world.

As I grabbed my Bible and began to read, these verses from Acts jumped out at me:

It shall come to pass in the last days, says God, that I will pour out of My Spirit on all flesh; your sons and your daughters shall prophesy, your young men shall see visions, your old men shall dream dreams. (2:17)

It shall come to pass that whoever calls on the name of the Lord shall be saved. (2:21)

Peter said to them, "Repent, and let every one of you be baptized in the name of Jesus Christ for the remission of sins; and you shall receive the gift of the Holy Spirit." (2:38)

Those who gladly received his word were baptized; and that day about three thousand souls were added to them. And they continued steadfastly in the apostles' doctrine and fellowship, in the breaking of bread, and in prayers. (2:41-42)

*All who believed were together, and had all things in
common. (2:44)*

*[They were] praising God and having favor with all the
people. And the Lord added to the church daily those who
were being saved. (2:47)*

The picture was becoming clear to me. Oswald Chambers
had lived, worked, and preached during the time of the
Holiness Movement. He was still a tutor in philosophy
at the Dunoon Training School, Scotland, when his
brother Arthur invited him to speak at his church in 1905.
And that's how and when Gertrude Hobbs met Oswald
Chambers.

I smiled in satisfaction. "Now, we're getting somewhere,"
I muttered.

Next question: In 1905, what did Gertrude Hobbs hear
when Oswald gave his message? His preaching inspired her
to believe that she was all God wanted her to be because of
her love for Jesus and that God could give her the power of
perfect love for God. Therefore, she would be empowered by
the Holy Spirit to obey God without fear. All she had to do
was to offer herself and completely surrender her life to God
because of what Jesus Christ had done for her on the cross.
And Jesus had said, "If you love Me, keep My command-
ments" (John 14:15).

Gertrude Hobbs was captivated by the message. She
knew in her heart exactly what she would do. She made her
decision.

Even though Gertrude Hobbs didn't take her ocean
voyage until 1908, God had a plan for her and for Oswald

Chambers. Together, they would love him and each other, and their lives would impact the world for all time.

The rest is history.

Kathleen told me many times, "My parents were really in love. There was no duty in the marriage."

Like mining for a precious metal, the difficulty in my efforts to discover the origins of this wonderful love story made the prize of my finding out more about Kathleen's parents even more precious.

The reward was to be pure gold from heaven, a deeper knowledge of Jesus Christ the Lord.

"Even today," I whispered, gently patting my Bible, "God never changes. He is from everlasting to everlasting, and we are safe in his care forever."

So far, so good. As I kept digging, I discovered that Oswald Chambers, a Baptist, became a close friend of Reader Harris, the founder of the Pentecostal League of Prayer:

> Reader Harris, after a distinguished career as a construction engineer in Bolivia, entered the legal profession, becoming a Queen's Counsel in 1894. By then, however, his deepest passion was for spiritual revival. From 1889 . . . he had a vision for spreading his new convictions. By the end of the century the emphases of Harris and the League were promoted by almost 150 networked local prayer groups throughout Britain with a total of 17,000 members.[3]

Sitting in Eltham Park Baptist Church, Gertrude Hobbs, who was many years younger than Oswald Chambers, forgot about her own life and the daily trials of Victorian England. Instead, she focused on the message of holiness and felt compelled to become part of the Pentecostal League of Prayer, which was "explicitly dedicated to praying for the filling of the Holy Spirit for all believers, for revival in the churches, and for the spread of scriptural holiness."[4] The League's perspective was that ecclesiastical distinctions were relatively unimportant: All denominations required the renewal that the Wesleyan experience offered.[5]

It seemed, then, that Oswald Chambers was an integral part of the Holiness Movement. His message was simple: Love Jesus Christ first, last, and always. He admonished believers to come away from beliefs *about* Jesus; instead, believe *in* Jesus and develop a close relationship with him.

Next question: What did the Holiness groups preach? This is what I found:

> Holiness is pervasive in the Bible. God called unto Himself a holy nation, set aside a holy priesthood, established a holy Sabbath, prescribed only holy sacrifices, to be done on a holy mount, in a holy Temple with a holy place—even a Holy of Holies. God himself is a holy God. And we are "called unto holiness." Without holiness no one shall see the Lord. God says, "I am holy; be ye holy." The Bible constantly and repeatedly calls for our total surrender to God in absolute consecration, for our complete submission to His will, for absolute obedience to His Word, and for separation from the defilement of sin of this world. Holiness is not only the essential characteristic of God's nature, it is the central emphasis of His Word. God is holy—we are to be holy too.
>
> Holiness is a Bible truth, not some denominational distinctive or pet doctrine of the Wesleyans, Nazarenes,

or Free Methodists. It was not invented to provide differentiation in the church marketplace. Holiness is biblical. And as a biblical truth it is sure to resurface. The Holy Spirit leads his people into all truth. The Holy Spirit will lead the church back to this biblical truth. It may be a while yet. It might come in different formats, with a changed language, and under a different heading, but it will resurface we know. Suppressing a Bible truth is like trying to hide a cork under water. Sooner or later it pops to the surface.[6]

Suppressing a Bible truth is like trying to hide a cork under water. Sooner or later it pops to the surface.

I reflected on the impact of this truth for the church today.

The message preached by Oswald Chambers was God's call to Gertrude. Her heart opened, and she obeyed.

$\mathscr{R}$ock

LONDON/BRITISH COLUMBIA
1995

> *They remembered that God was their rock, and the*
> *Most High God their Redeemer.*   PSALM 78:35

"Hi, Kathleen! It's me again." I waited for Kathleen to speak.

"I know," she chuckled.

"I am so excited about everything I am finding out about your mother. I really believe that her life is a terrific role model for women today who want a closer relationship with Jesus Christ." I paused. "Do you use the word *terrific* in England?"

"Yes," she replied, with her typical good nature.

"Okay. Good. Is now a good time to ask you some more questions about your mother and when she lived and so forth?"

"Yes."

"Thanks! I've been wondering what your mother would

have worn and how her hair would have been fixed and things like that."

"The styles were very prim—"

"Excuse me for interrupting, but *prim*? What did that look like?"

With her usual aplomb, Kathleen continued, "Some might call the styles prudish or straitlaced, but by today's standards, women's styles at that time would be considered formal. The clothes had high collars and long skirts, and women wore their hair in an upsweep. My mother loved nice clothes, but she seldom had a chance to get any. They were nearly always out of her reach financially. She often talked about 'how elegantly American women were shod.'"

I was taking notes as fast as I could. "I wish I could take shorthand like your mother did," I interjected.

Kathleen continued, "My mother adored the sea and always went out with the fishermen at five in the morning for the first catch—"

"Just like the virtuous wife in Proverbs!"

"She was never seasick, except for one occasion when we were coming back from a holiday in Ireland. The English Channel is well known for its violent currents, and much to my mother's humiliation, she was sick then, but never on an ocean liner."

Kathleen was giving me really solid information, so I decided I wouldn't interrupt anymore and would try to put it together later. I kept taking notes.

"One thing I do recall: My mother always said, 'God's purposes are always fulfilled.' My father said that, too, and that is probably why my mother was able to live the way she did. She had faith in the Almighty. I do too. They trusted

God for everything. Money was not important, or success, or self-promotion. Devotion to Jesus Christ was everything."

"I wish I could write faster, Kathleen. How about a tape recorder? Could we look into that?"

"I'll see what I can do," she replied.

All too soon, we had to end the conversation.

"So, Kathleen, you're going to write to me and send me some stuff, right?"

"I will write," she laughed, "and send you some *stuff*, Ducks."

After hanging up the phone, I began thinking as fast as I could. Kathleen did not recall circumstances in chronological order. Instead, she remembered events in order of priority. But she did make the past come alive. I just wondered how I would ever get all the information into the proper order.

Most of all, I appreciated Kathleen's sincere friendship. She lived in the power of Jesus Christ, and it showed in everything she did, not only for me but for everyone she met. She reminded me that faith is the key—not faith in ourselves but faith in the power of almighty God, through believing that Jesus Christ is who he says he is.

She told me once that when someone asked her father if the story about Jesus was true, he replied, "Yes."

The person responded, "I don't believe it."

Oswald answered, "Just because you don't believe it doesn't mean it isn't true."

Kathleen always said her mother and father lived by faith in God.

Someone told me once that the Greek word for faith can be translated "conviction," "confidence," "trust," and "belief." And the Bible considers faith a shield of protection:

"Above all, [take] the shield of faith with which you will be able to quench all the fiery darts of the wicked one" (Ephesians 6:16).

I had learned that the Holiness Movement encouraged believers to live by faith. If it is true that writers reflect their times, then that special time of Andrew Murray, Reader Harris, Oswald Chambers, Biddy Chambers, and many others all over the world reflected the glory of God. And Kathleen carried it into her generation.

I dare to believe that with God's help we can continue forever the stream of living water that flows right from the throne.

Women today have a great opportunity to be lights in the great darkness of social anxiety, spiritual disillusionment, and global turmoil. In our homes, workplaces, neighborhoods, even as we walk down the street, we can share God's love if we believe in the power of Jesus Christ. Was he who he said he was?

He still is.

And our lives reveal that truth as we walk in faith.

I was reminded of the verse that says, "I will come in the strength and with the mighty acts of the Lord God; I will mention and praise Your righteousness, even Yours alone" (Psalm 71:16, AMP).

I felt deep in my heart that Kathleen Chambers was revealing the mystery of relinquishment of oneself to almighty God. She told me that we need not only to have faith but to be *faithful*. She pointed out to me more than once the deep bond of love between her father and her mother and, for both of them, their absolute surrender of their lives to God.

I wondered, did Kathleen's grandmother make the

marriage match by inviting Oswald to accompany Gertrude on the ocean voyage to the United States? Yes and no. She may have asked the favor, but it was because she was an instrument in God's divine orchestration. The Bible tells us that God's gift to a good man is a good woman: "Houses and riches are an inheritance from fathers, but a prudent wife is from the LORD" (Proverbs 19:14).

Not only was Oswald a good man, he was God's man. During his studies at Dunoon Training College, he wrote to his father, "Let my whole life be the answer, for the sake of the wounded palms and feet of the Savior of the world." Biddy had the same heart and love for Jesus. The Bible says that "an excellent wife is the crown of her husband" (Proverbs 12:4). Therefore, it seems that God knew exactly what he was doing when he brought Biddy and Oswald together.

When Oswald Chambers met Gertrude Hobbs, she was feminine, sturdy, delightful, and virtuous. With other family members, she rode her bicycle into the country on weekends. Entertainment consisted of dinners with others (Oswald was invited) and going for long walks. She loved to play tennis and belonged to a club where she played whenever possible.

Music was always important to Gertrude. In the winter she attended classical concerts as often as she could. She played the piano and often enjoyed musical evenings with her family.

Was there any question that Gertrude Hobbs would be a suitable wife for Oswald Chambers? Their marriage, their life together, was based on the Rock, the solid foundation of Jesus Christ. They would not fail because they depended on God for everything. "He who finds a wife finds a good thing, and obtains favor from the LORD" (Proverbs 18:22).

I remembered that Kathleen always said, "God fulfills his promises. He always provides the way—with or without our help."

"God's order in the haphazard," I wrote down on my notepad.

It occurred to me, then, that Jesus Christ is the Rock on which everything (including little old me) stands, and that without him, we can do nothing.

I had heard that this idea was also called worm theology, and I wanted to explore the notion further.

I grabbed my phone and made a call to my pastor's wife.

"What is worm theology?"

She said, "Some people think worm theology goes a bit too far—putting yourself lower than God would want you to, because we are, after all, the children of the King." She said that when she was a small child, she heard a preacher praying, "Make me a worm."

"What does that mean?"

She replied, "I'm not certain what it means. Some people think of it as being humble. I've never called myself a worm, but maybe it's a good idea. I was only a little girl when I heard about it. I think it's in a hymn."

"How does that relate to the fact that Jesus is the Rock on which we stand?"

"I have no idea."

We spent the next hour talking about being a worm, and she found a hymn where it was mentioned—"Alas! and Did My Savior Bleed," by Isaac Watts (1674–1748).

I began to realize that God loves worms, too—just as he does the lilies of the field.

After our talk, I decided to get back to thinking about a rock. Jesus was, and is, the Rock on which everything is built—and Oswald, Biddy, and Kathleen believed this truth. They lived it.

Jesus said, "Whoever hears these sayings of Mine, and does them, I will liken him to a wise man who built his house on the rock: and the rain descended, the floods came, and the winds blew and beat on that house; and it did not fall, for it was founded on the rock. But everyone who hears these sayings of Mine, and does not do them, will be like a foolish man who built his house on the sand: and the rain descended, the floods came, and the winds blew and beat on that house; and it fell. And great was its fall" (Matthew 7:24-27).

Whenever I talked with Kathleen, I felt lifted up to Jesus, the Rock of our salvation. Kathleen's holiness shone in everything she did. It was expressed with delight and a sense of humor. She told me that her father was sometimes referred to as an irreverent reverend because he laughed and joked.

Kathleen informed me that holiness and humor walk hand in hand: That's why Kathleen wanted me to write her mother's story. She said she had read my books and thought they were funny.

So much for my ego about being a writer. But the Chamberses' love of life flowed through her comment to me: "Be patient, Ducks!"

Kathleen lived through two world wars, bombings, and poverty, but she followed her mother's lead, and her faith in God held. Kathleen lost her father when she was four years old, but she never lost her father's teaching. Because Biddy Chambers kept the faith and was faithful to the foundation of our faith, Jesus Christ, Kathleen never forgot what she learned as a tiny girl. Even long after both of Kathleen's parents were in heaven, Kathleen's faith, built on the Rock, held steady against the winds and waves of life's difficulties, even when spiritual apathy surrounded her.

Her memories, shared from her heart through letters and telephone conversations, tell the tale of ordinary people made extraordinary by God's grace and then used for his glory.

Kathleen told me that Oswald often said that one life given to God could impact history. Little did Gertrude Hobbs realize that hers would be such a life.

The legacy that was Kathleen's is ours today. Jesus is not a religion. Then and now, the Son of God is available to everyone. The work of the Cross continues until Jesus comes again.

Although Kathleen was in her eighties, she lived the truth of Psalm 92:12-14: "The godly will flourish like palm trees and grow strong like the cedars of Lebanon. For they are transplanted to the LORD's own house. They flourish in the courts of our God. Even in old age they will still produce fruit; they will remain vital and green" (NLT).

As I wrote this, right then and there I prayed, *Please, God, do this manuscript your way.*

Could that have been considered a wormlike thought? No matter. I felt peace take over my soul. I was no longer concerned about time frames, chronology, or the method of getting it all down. I realized that the chronicle that came through the life of Biddy Chambers was the narrative that we never tire of telling, the one that is best described in the familiar hymn "I Love to Tell the Story," some of which follows:

I love to tell the story of unseen things above,
Of Jesus and His glory, of Jesus and His love;

I love to tell the story because I know 'tis true,
It satisfies my longings as nothing else can do.

I love to tell the story!
'Twill be my theme in glory—
To tell the old, old story
Of Jesus and His love.[1]

Thinking about Jesus' being the Rock gave me great comfort throughout the rest of the day while I cleaned and cooked and did a little work in the garden, where I came across a sweet little worm and decided I would name him—Wormy. Then, I left him to God.

> *O*swald and Biddy Chambers were ordinary people made extraordinary by God's grace and then used for his glory.

I went in the house, found a well-known hymn, played it on my piano, and sang it out loud in the living room, where the picture window faced the garden. I hoped Wormy liked it.

The Church's one foundation is Jesus Christ her Lord;
She is His new creation by water and the word.
From heaven He came and sought her to be His holy bride;
With His own blood He bought her, and for her life He died.

Elect from every nation, yet one o'er all the earth;
Her charter of salvation, one Lord, one faith, one birth;

One holy name she blesses, partakes one holy food,
And to one hope she presses, with every grace endued.

Mid toil and tribulation, and tumult of her war,
She waits the consummation of peace forevermore;
Till, with the vision glorious, her longing eyes are blest,
And the great Church victorious shall be the Church
at rest.

Yet she on earth hath union with God the Three in One,
And mystic sweet communion with those whose rest
is won.
O happy ones and holy! Lord, give us grace that we,
Like them, the meek and lowly, on high may dwell
with Thee.²

While I played the piano and sang, I could almost imagine what it must have been like to be in the company of those precious believers back in the time of the Holiness Movement. *Can it be like that today?* I wondered.

Later, after the day's work was done, I went outside to enjoy the evening air. I hoped to find Wormy again and even took my flashlight out to look for the little fellow. Somehow, I knew that he would understand how I was feeling. But I could not find him.

I did see something else, though. I looked up at the night sky, brilliantly lit by twinkling stars, and thought of Psalm 19:1: "The heavens proclaim the glory of God. The skies display his craftsmanship" (NLT). I could see the North Star, by which sailors navigated. Without that star to guide them, ships could become hopelessly off course and be lost or even destroyed.

Jesus Christ, our Rock and our Foundation, is our North

Star. We can count on him to guide us safely in this life, and in the next.

Oswald and Biddy were already with God.

And one day, we would meet.

$\mathcal{K}$athleen

NEW YORK/ENGLAND
1908

> *"I know the plans I have for you," says the LORD.*
> *"They are plans for good and not for disaster, to give*
> *you a future and a hope. In those days when you*
> *pray, I will listen. If you look for me wholeheartedly,*
> *you will find me."* JEREMIAH 29:11-13, NLT

In the year of our Lord 1908, when Gertrude Hobbs sailed
across the ocean from England to visit her faithful friend
Marian and to see about a job in the United States, she felt
loved by her mother, who had asked Oswald to look after
her daughter on the voyage, and upheld by God, in whom
Gertrude had placed her complete trust.

Standing on the deck of the ocean liner headed for the
United States delighted Gertrude. What an opportunity! She
scanned the horizon eagerly. She knew she would not see
land for a long time. But she was unconcerned. She loved

the sea. Her sea legs were steady, and she gazed straight ahead while her heart trusted God.

Sailing away to a new country and the possibility of a new position of employment excited her. The fact that she was accompanied by a man she admired was more than icing on the cake. Thinking about it was a bit overwhelming.

"Miss Hobbs?" Oswald appeared at her side.

"Mr. Chambers! What a surprise!"

They both laughed heartily. After a pleasant walk around the area of the ship allowed for the passengers, they retired to their respective quarters and private thoughts.

Oswald was on his way to the United States to preach and teach wherever, and whenever, his heavenly Father planned. Only God and Oswald knew what was in the young man's heart.

Did he long for a wife?

Meanwhile, Gertrude Hobbs trusted God completely for each day and for her future. If she had thoughts of marrying Oswald Chambers, she kept them to herself.

The next morning she rose early, as was her custom, dressed quickly, and hurried on deck to enjoy the sunrise. She was especially fond of nature and never missed a chance to view the sky at dawn, at dusk, throughout the day, and especially after a rainfall. Rainbows always reminded her of God's promise to Noah: "The rainbow shall be in the cloud, and I will look on it to remember the everlasting covenant between God and every living creature of all flesh that is on the earth" (Genesis 9:16).

The moon, the sun, the stars, and even clouds lifted her heart to God. She stood in awe of his greatness. Gazing out on the vast ocean that he had created, she felt a reverent fear of his power, and she was glad to have a heavenly Father who loved her. If he could create the sun and the stars, could he not also order her life to be one filled with his joy?

Standing on the deck, she remembered with pleasure the last time she and Marian had stood looking at a rainbow, not too long before Marian decided to go to America.

"It's God's promise to be with me," Marian had whispered softly, gazing at the glorious display of color arching over the earth.

"His promise to be with us all, wherever we are," Gertrude replied, giving her friend a quick hug. "I will miss you, Marian."

"Miss Hobbs?"

"Oh!" Gertrude broke out in laughter. "Mr. Chambers, you startled me!"

Completely engrossed in her thoughts, Gertrude had failed to hear Oswald's footsteps on the deck.

"May I join you?" It seemed that Oswald, too, loved to watch the sunrise.

"Yes, yes, of course," she replied enthusiastically. "I love to watch the sun scatter silk threads of color across the sky."

Delighted with her response, Oswald began telling her about his own love of nature, and about his studies at Dunoon, and the purpose of his trip to continue his work in the Holiness Movement. Most of all, he began to share his faith.

He told her about sitting under the preaching of F. B. Meyer, "a saintly man," and one gifted of God. Then Oswald related his experience at Dunoon. "In a flash something happened inside me, and I saw that I had been wanting power in my own hand, so to speak, that I might say—Look what I have by putting my all on the altar."

Oswald went on to say that "when you know what God has done for you, the power and tyranny of sin is gone, and the radiant, unspeakable emancipation of the indwelling Christ has come."[1]

Gertrude stood quietly, listening to every word.

"You know," Oswald suddenly stated, "I have a sister named Gertrude."

"Yes, I know," she answered with amusement. "That is my first name too."

"Miss Hobbs, would you allow me to call you by a nickname?"

"Gertie?" She grinned.

"No," Oswald answered quickly.

"What then?"

"Beloved Disciple."

Gertrude's gentle smile covered her soaring heart. "Of course," she answered easily. "But only if I may call you Oswald."

"Agreed, B. D.," he heartily responded.

And so it was done. To Oswald Chambers, Gertrude Hobbs was "Beloved Disciple." Quickly pronounced, the letters *B. D.* sounded like "Biddy."

"The sun is up," he offered.

"So it is," she replied. "And I have work to do. Please excuse me."

Biddy needed some time to herself to digest what had just happened.

Did *beloved* mean "dearly loved"? Was Oswald telling her something? She quickly dismissed the thought. Walking resolutely toward her quarters to prepare for the morning meal, she whispered quietly, "God knows."

Biddy trusted God and experienced the peace that passes

all understanding. By the time the trip ended, the journey into a new life had begun for Biddy. Oswald wrote her letters from God's Bible School, in Cincinnati, Ohio, and from Maine, where he was preaching.

Biddy waited eagerly for Oswald to lead the way.

Oswald returned to England to continue his work with the League of Prayer, while Biddy stayed in New York to complete her time on the job.

Were God's plans good? Oswald was back across the ocean, and she was still far away in New York. Biddy might have wondered about that. She continued to trust God, however, while Oswald did all of the appropriate things that thrill the heart of a woman cherished by a man who sets her above all others.

"Miss Hobbs, would you allow me to call you by a nickname?" "Gertie?" She grinned. "No," Oswald answered quickly. "What then?" "Beloved Disciple."

As autumn changed leaves from green to red and gold, Oswald wrote to Mrs. Hobbs, Biddy's mother, and declared his love for her daughter. Gertrude was about twenty-four years old when he looked after her on the voyage in 1908. He was thirty-four. By the end of October 1908, he had notified her mother and his parents of his serious intentions.

In her heart, Biddy already knew.

Of course, there were financial concerns on the part of family members and others who knew Oswald. Did he purpose to become rich in material wealth? No. Oswald Chambers believed in God's resources and in laying up treasures in heaven. He had no regular income. He also had a habit of giving away his last shilling. How would he, a wandering preacher, take care of a wife?

Oswald knew that God knew, and Biddy knew that Oswald and God knew, and in that knowing they sailed securely ahead into the future God had planned for them.

When Biddy returned to England from the United States in November 1908, Oswald was waiting for her with a proposal of marriage.

She accepted. A two-year engagement would follow.

Oswald's Beloved Disciple (B. D.), Biddy, was now officially Oswald's "dearly beloved."

Oswald left to travel extensively for the League of Prayer. Biddy didn't see much of him for a while, but they corresponded regularly. She loved Oswald, and she loved Jesus Christ. Therefore, her heart was at rest as she patiently waited for Oswald to return and for God to order their life together.

Biddy wholeheartedly supported Oswald's work with the League of Prayer. She accepted and honored God's call on her life.

"Who can find a virtuous wife? For her worth is far above rubies. The heart of her husband safely trusts her; so he will have no lack of gain. She does him good and not evil all the days of her life" (Proverbs 31:10-12).

Oswald could trust his future wife. Only God knew what that trust would mean for their future.

Following the teaching of the Bible, Biddy was *in* the world, but not *of* the world. Her good deeds were known to many as she quietly went about her daily duties. She didn't complain. Instead, she fought the good fight of faith, allowing Jesus Christ to shine through her.

Miss Gertrude Hobbs (B. D.) had her feet planted firmly in the heavenlies while she walked the earth. She traveled steadily in the light of Jesus Christ, as described by the apostle Paul:

> *We keep on praying for you, asking our God to enable you to live a life worthy of his call. May he give you the power to accomplish all the good things your faith prompts you to do. Then the name of our Lord Jesus will be honored because of the way you live, and you will be honored along with him. This is all made possible because of the grace of our God and Lord, Jesus Christ.*
>
> 2 THESSALONIANS 1:11-12 (NLT)

Because Biddy trusted Jesus Christ and put her complete faith in him, she waited for the Holy Spirit to guide each step. She believed her Bible when she read, "Trust in the LORD with all your heart, and lean not on your own understanding" (Proverbs 3:5).

In 1909, while Gertrude Hobbs was planning her wedding to Oswald Chambers, there was great unrest among women of the world, especially in her home country, England.

In the middle of the nineteenth century, when the women's suffrage movement began, women not only wanted the right to vote but desired better education for girls, and they were ready to use any methods available to promote their cause.

At that time, as it is in our modern world, not all women shared the same views.

How did God's children respond? Again, not everyone felt the same way.

At first, the women were peaceful, writing letters to Parliament and organizing petitions. But these attempts had no effect on the rights of women. Tired of waiting, Emmeline Parkhurst, the founder of the Women's Social and Political Union, decided it was time for stronger tactics. As women followed her lead, they broke windows and committed arson and bombings to draw attention to their cause.

The suffragettes marched through the streets and wrote inscriptions on walls. Many of them went to prison, where they refused to eat.[2] In one eighteen-month period, Emmeline Parkhurst endured ten hunger strikes, which often resulted in force feeding, a horrible and painful ordeal.

While Emmeline Parkhurst was becoming famous for her tactics and became a famous author, Gertrude Hobbs quietly went about her daily duties. Did anyone but God know who she was? He knew, and it was enough, because he had plans for her future—good plans.

Meanwhile, Biddy waited on God. Peace, not conflict, would be the result in her life.

On May 25 in the year of our Lord 1910, Miss Gertrude Hobbs married Oswald Chambers at the Eltham Park church. Then the newly married couple traveled back to America, where they spent their time at camp meetings. They stayed with various believers and were called "God's elect" by those families who felt privileged to offer them food and rest for their physical well-being.

Mr. and Mrs. Chambers, on the other hand, provided spiritual food from the deep fountain of Bible truth that nourished the soul.

Biddy was known as a gracious and gifted lady. She displayed the same qualities as Ruth, wife of Boaz, in the Old Testament: "All the people of my town know that you are a virtuous woman" (Ruth 3:11). Like Ruth and the virtuous wife in Proverbs 31, B. D. was an asset to her husband.

Members of the League of Prayer were hoping for and praying about establishing a place of spiritual training in England. They knew that Oswald would be an excellent principal and that Biddy would be a positive influence on the students.

Early in December 1910, a large house became available on Northside, Clapham Common, London. Things moved rapidly, and within a very short time, Oswald and Biddy moved in and prepared to welcome the first resident students.

By 1911, the location had become known as the Bible Training College. The building was perfectly suited for the purpose. There was a large, double drawing room that could serve quite nicely as the lecture hall, and the structure could house about twenty-five students. Mr. Chambers was the principal, and Mrs. Chambers was the lady superintendent. When funds were low, they offered correspondence classes.

Oswald often said, "I never see my way. I know the God who guides so I fear nothing. I never have farseeing plans, only confident trust." The couple's foundation was faith and prayer as they walked "by faith, not by sight" (2 Corinthians 5:7).

One by one, eager learners appeared. The students

shared meals, everyday tasks, and friendship as they lived and worked together.

Biddy Chambers was also a featured speaker at the Pentecostal League of Prayer meetings, which were part of the transdenominational British Wesleyan–Holiness Movement.

Before the wedding, Oswald Chambers, a Baptist, had become a close friend of Reader Harris. Mrs. Harris and the Harrises' daughter played prominent roles in the League of Prayer, so it was no surprise that after Oswald and Biddy married, Biddy Chambers would become a League speaker.

Biddy used her training as a stenographer and her rapid shorthand speed to record Oswald's lectures. Did she ever imagine those transcribed words would be read by millions?

B. D. was a Beloved Disciple and a faithful, loving wife. Because her goal was to be attentive during Oswald's preaching, his words would impact the world for Jesus Christ.

Oswald taught that holiness is a gift from God. "God makes us holy. He sanctifies. He does it all. All I have to do is to let go of my right to myself."

He based his teaching on Romans 12:1-2: "I beseech you therefore, brethren, by the mercies of God, that ye present your bodies a living sacrifice, holy, acceptable unto God, which is your reasonable service. And be not conformed to this world: but be ye transformed by the renewing of your mind, that ye may prove what is that good, and acceptable, and perfect, will of God" (KJV).

Oswald preached over and over, "It is not *do, do,* and you'll *be* with the Lord. It is *be, be,* and I will *do* through you." Both letting go of self and relying entirely on God were imperative. Oswald and Biddy practiced what he preached. Together, they purposed for God, and God used them for his purposes.

At the crack of dawn, students at the Bible college were awakened by the sound of Oswald playing the piano and singing one of his favorite hymns:

When morning gilds the skies,
My heart awaking cries,
May Jesus Christ be praised!
Alike at work and prayer,
To Jesus I repair:
May Jesus Christ be praised!

The night becomes as day,
When from the heart we say,
May Jesus Christ be praised!
The powers of darkness fear
When this sweet chant they hear,
May Jesus Christ be praised!

Ye nations of mankind,
In this your concord find,
May Jesus Christ be praised!
Let all the earth around
Ring joyous with the sound,
May Jesus Christ be praised!

Be this, while life is mine,
My canticle divine,
May Jesus Christ be praised!
Sing this th' eternal song
Through all the ages long,
May Jesus Christ be praised![3]

In the meantime, the wonderful aroma of sausage and eggs filled the air, promising food for the body as well as for the soul. In addition to Biddy's other qualifications as a worthy wife, she was also an excellent cook, bringing to mind Proverbs 31:15: "She also rises while it is yet night, and provides food for her household."

When Mrs. Chambers was expecting their first and only child, she was cautious. Infant deaths were quite common in 1913. On May 24, 1913, after a difficult labor, Oswald and Biddy's daughter was born at the Bible college. They named their newborn Kathleen, from a Greek word that means "pure," "most excellent," and "finest." She was their "Little Flower of God," God's gift to Oswald and Biddy Chambers.

In the early 1900s, a lack of cleanliness was a major factor in many infant deaths. But Mrs. Chambers was an excellent housekeeper. She studied the best way to care for Kathleen and implemented healthy hygiene, as well as good feeding practices. And because of Biddy's first-rate care, baby Kathleen was not included in the statistics for the high infant death rate.

Biddy Chambers was a prudent and watchful mother. She was prepared, and her husband blessed her. The students loved tiny Kathleen. Oswald carried her everywhere. Her birth completed the picture of harmony at the Bible college.

Kathleen would be barely walking in 1914, the year that marked the beginning of the First World War.

What would God do with Kathleen?

TEN

$\mathcal{N}$iche

LONDON/BRITISH COLUMBIA
1995

> *Those who live in the shelter of the Most High*
> *will find rest in the shadow of the Almighty. This*
> *I declare about the LORD: He alone is my refuge,*
> *my place of safety; he is my God, and I trust him.*

PSALM 91:1-2, NLT

"Kathleen, do you remember the Bible Training College in England?" I was on the phone again with this dear person who now allowed me to consider her a friend.

There was silence from her end of the connection.

Quickly I continued, "I mean, I know you were born there, but babies don't remember much."

"I can tell you many things about it. I am just looking for something my mother told me about. I have it written down. Excuse me—can you wait for a moment?" Kathleen was always polite and very considerate.

I had all the time in the world.

We spoke briefly, however, because Lady, her dog, summoned her to go for a walk. "Nature calls," Kathleen chuckled. "I'll find the information and send it to you in a letter. I also want to send you some writing of my mother's."

"Okay, then," I said, smiling to myself, "I'll be anxious to hear from you. I just love your letters, and thank you."

As friends do, Kathleen and I had begun to share the happenings in our daily lives, and that included our dogs.

Lady (Kathleen sent me a photo) was a breed I didn't recognize. She was medium size, was mostly white, had short fur, was brown on her ears and face, and had a slightly curved tail. She looked very friendly. I never did find out what type of dog Lady was. It didn't matter, anyway. Because Kathleen loved Lady, I did too.

My dog, Cookie, a toy poodle crossed with Pomeranian (today he would be called a Pomapoo), was tiny in stature but big in heart. He was called Cookie because as a puppy he could be held in one's palm, and his fluffy fur (sort of beige) made his big dark eyes and black nose appear like chocolate chips in a chocolate-chip cookie.

Clear across the Atlantic, our dogs communicated too. Cookie would bark on the telephone, and Lady would listen.

As Kathleen would say, "Didn't Jesus love animals too?"

When our phone conversation ended, I began searching for the word *niche*. I was looking for it because Kathleen had written that her father talked about our "niche."

She said he often stated that if we were loyal to Jesus Christ, we would find our "niche" in life and know how best to serve God.

For starters, I had to call a person or two to find out exactly how to pronounce it: "Is it 'nitch,' or 'n-e-e-e-sh'?"

"How do you spell it?"

"N-i-c-h-e."

"I'll get back to you."

Waiting, waiting, always waiting, I said to myself, hanging up the telephone receiver. I decided to find out more for myself.

The next stop, a dictionary, said that a niche was sort of like a nest.

While I was flipping pages to find *nest,* another person phoned to chat, and when I asked her how to say my new word, she said, "I know how it should sound because that's where I'm going to be put, next to my husband, when I die—in a niche," she said, pronouncing it "n-e-e-e-sh."

"Thanks a lot!" I said sincerely, hanging up the receiver.

"Okay. Now I can pronounce it. *N-e-e-e-sh,*" I said, still searching for *nest.*

Nest, on the other hand, means not just a safe place for the young, such as baby birds, but also "a place of rest, retreat, or lodging."[1] "Ah, so that's why they say when children leave home it is an empty *nest.*"

Dimly I recalled that the psalms talk about safety and refuge, and I figured that meant God's nest.

Interesting, but back to more about *niche.*

I made one more phone call to someone I knew who had once lived in England. Perhaps it had a particular meaning on that side of the pond. "What does *niche* mean?"

"Oh," she laughed. "In England we would call that a hidey-hole."

"That sounds very comfortable," I replied. "Thank you."

"Anytime," she responded. "See you." At that point, I decided to try to find a specific psalm that talks about refuge or safety. Using my Bible concordance, I found Psalm 91.

After reading it, I copied it down because I wanted to be able to bounce it off Kathleen and see what she thought of the whole concept. I used the King James Version because it was Kathleen's favorite.

I was so happy to have found that psalm, and it brought me such peace, that I stuck it up on the wall right over my desk.

> He that dwelleth in the secret place of the most
>   High shall abide under the shadow of the
>   Almighty.
> I will say of the LORD, He is my refuge and my
>   fortress: my God; in him will I trust.
> Surely he shall deliver thee from the snare of the
>   fowler, and from the noisome pestilence.
> He shall cover thee with his feathers, and under
>   his wings shalt thou trust: his truth shall be
>   thy shield and buckler.
> Thou shalt not be afraid for the terror by night;
>   nor for the arrow that flieth by day;
> Nor for the pestilence that walketh in darkness;
>   nor for the destruction that wasteth at
>   noonday.
> A thousand shall fall at thy side, and ten
>   thousand at thy right hand; but it shall not
>   come nigh thee.
> Only with thine eyes shalt thou behold and see
>   the reward of the wicked.

Because thou hast made the Lord, *which is my*
  refuge, even the most High, thy habitation;
There shall no evil befall thee, neither shall any
  plague come nigh thy dwelling.
For he shall give his angels charge over thee, to
  keep thee in all thy ways.
They shall bear thee up in their hands, lest thou
  dash thy foot against a stone.
Thou shalt tread upon the lion and adder:
  the young lion and the dragon shalt thou
  trample under feet.
Because he hath set his love upon me, therefore
  will I deliver him: I will set him on high,
  because he hath known my name.
He shall call upon me, and I will answer him:
  I will be with him in trouble; I will deliver
  him, and honour him.
With long life will I satisfy him, and shew him
  my salvation.

I just had to call Kathleen and tell her what I had discovered.

"Did I wake you?"

"It is all right," she said.

"Guess what?"

"What?"

"Well, a niche is like a nest, and a nest is for baby birds, and baby birds are kept safe until ready to fly—"

For once, Kathleen interrupted. "Until they are pushed out of the nest. Mother eagles do that, you know—push the eaglets out of the nest and into thin air.

"I have put some material in the mail for you about my mother. Please let me know when you receive it."

"Thank you, Kathleen. I will."

After a long walk to look for birds' nests, I came to the conclusion that the psalm means that we can live in the nest and we will be kept safe by almighty God.

"But what about flying?" I wondered out loud as I went back into the house.

Careful searching led me to ascertain that God compares the way he trains and cares for his people to the way an eagle watches over and trains its young: "An eagle stirs up its nest, hovers over its young, spreading out its wings, taking them up, carrying them on its wings" (Deuteronomy 32:11). Much later, a friend told me that if the eaglet fails to fly, the parent will swoop down at the last minute, fly beneath the eaglet and catch it on its back, and carry it back to the nest for another lesson.

I concluded that the Bible was correct. If one lived "in the secret place of the Most High," in God's nest (niche), then one would always be safe.

I decided the concept of flying was beyond my understanding at that point. Flying would have to wait.

A few days later, just as Kathleen had promised, I received a most welcome letter. And wouldn't you know? The information taught me a lot about how to be one who "dwelleth" in a *niche*.

Again Kathleen apologized for her "awful handwriting." She wrote,

> *My mother got up early and prayed. She shorthanded all her prayers down in an exercise book, then threw them away when the book was filled up. She didn't shut herself away. When children were staying with us, they would wander all over the house, and my mother would immediately go with them. They called her "Mrs. Biddy."*

We always had dogs and cats. We'd walk the dogs and have long conversations with both of them.

Our dog Peter was a great personality. Our next door neighbors would ring up and say, "Can Peter come to tea?" And my mother would open the front door and say, "Go to tea," and Peter would go immediately. The same performance would be followed when he came back an hour later.

Letter writing was very important to my mother, and her letters were always special. She would always write words to people who were going on journeys. Even if short, her notes were always treasured.

Some odds and ends about Mother's interests. She went each year to the Academy for the exhibition of artists' new portraits and landscapes. The Academy is in the heart of London. I usually went with her.

Each summer in July there is a nightly classical concert in our Albert Hall.

What is Albert Hall? I wondered as I wandered through various texts for photographs.

What I found was outstanding. Like other buildings in England, the architecture was majestic and stately. I could understand the title of "The Royal Albert Hall of Arts and Sciences." It opened March 29, 1871. I even found an illustration of the grand-opening ceremony.

Located in London, in the South Kensington area, the hall accommodates the largest pipe organ in the United Kingdom.

Full of anticipation, I returned to Kathleen's letter.

The Hall was built in Queen Victoria's reign in memory of her beloved Prince Albert. It's to interest ordinary people in classical music, and hundreds of people go there each night.

Most people stand for three to three and a half hours, on the floor of the Hall. It holds hundreds of people, and is full every evening.

I went with my mother at least four times a week. She had a seat.

Famous conductors are there each night, along with famous orchestras.

Sir Henry Wood, an English conductor, started these concerts after the First World War. They are known as the Promenade Concerts.

I had to stop in order to learn about the Promenade Concerts and Sir Henry Wood.

Sir Henry (1869–1944) founded the Promenade Concerts in 1895 and conducted them for about fifty years. He was knighted in 1911 for his work.

Today, the concerts (which have an eight-week summer season of daily orchestral classical music performances) are known as the BBC Proms or The Sir Henry Wood Promenade Concerts (presented by the BBC). The Proms are the biggest classical music festival in the world. People still stand (no charge), and some walk around (that's why it is called a promenade), but reserved seats are also available for those who care to purchase tickets.

"Just think," I said softly to my dog, "Royal Albert Hall still stands today, and Biddy Chambers was part of those concerts. She even had a reserved seat!"

Cookie rolled over in his cozy bed and went to sleep.

Once I had made the decision not to worry about time and chronology, it was much easier for me to learn about Biddy Chambers from Kathleen. Every nugget of information was another puzzle piece in the portrait of her mother.

Her letter continued, *In Muswell Hill*—

What was Muswell Hill? Back to the books. After all, phone calls were expensive, and I couldn't expect Kathleen to explain everything.

Here's what I found: Muswell Hill, London, where Kathleen lived, was known as a "slice of old England," a charming Edwardian suburb in north London.

The earliest records show that it originated in the twelfth century. When land was granted to a newly formed order of nuns, a chapel was built on the site, called "Our Ladie of Muswell."

The story behind the name Muswell (the "Mossy Well") began with a "miracle" from a natural spring or well that was said to have miraculous properties. It seems a Scottish king was cured of disease after drinking the water of the spring. As a result, the area became a stop for traveling pilgrims during medieval times.

I knew I was getting carried away, but I was thinking about the woman of Samaria who gave Jesus a drink of water from a well, and of the wellspring of God's love that we can experience in our lives only as his gift.

Then I finished reading Kathleen's letter.

In Muswell Hill there were organ recitals each week in our lovely old church, St. James, and my mother always went to listen, midday for an hour.

My mother was a very political animal and read the Daily Telegraph *daily. She had all Churchill's war books and admired him tremendously although she was really liberal. She read all kinds of books and loved novels, adventures, and history.*

She was a great admirer of R. L. Stevenson and had

copies of all of his books. She read widely and enjoyed both poetry and prose.

My mother's deafness could have been a real problem, but she made light of it and laughed.

But other people's attitude to deafness is extraordinary. They behave as if deafness is synonymous with a mental condition. Having hearing aids accentuates every noise, making meal times very aggravating and exhausting.

She would never lip-read because she said most people's mouths are not always particularly well looked after and bits of food sit in corners of lips. . . . All these things are important to my mother as a person.

I recalled what Kathleen had shared with me about her mother's childhood. Gertrude Hobbs's constant ill health forced her to miss most of the required formal education in her home country, England, and had seriously impaired her hearing.

I never did ask Kathleen if it was just at mealtimes that Biddy did not read lips. I felt that would have been an intrusion into her privacy. But I could see her mother's point!

In our conversations and letters, Kathleen taught me that holiness was not something we achieve; it is God's gift, and that is how we dwell in the safety of God's love and power. She explained it this way: "The simple life of a child trusts."

"Is that all?" I asked in my ignorance.

She never pointed out my shortcomings and the immaturity of my faith. Instead, she patiently explained that her father taught, and her mother lived, the natural life of God's child. It is all about God, not us. "God does it all," she said.

"All we have to do is to *believe* it. We have to let go of our right to ourselves and completely trust God for everything. That is how the books came to be.

"My mother was never hurried; she was relaxed, and she often said, 'Let's see what God does next.'

"Life was not easy for my mother. She had to fight for everything, but her life was hid with Christ in God."

I realized that Biddy Chambers lived the life outlined in the Bible: "You died, and your life is hidden with Christ in God" (Colossians 3:3).

I began to understand. God as our refuge meant we could live in the shadow of the Almighty, but we could not see him in our present state. A favorite hymn sung at the Bible Training College explained it best:

> *Immortal, invisible, God only wise,*
> *In light inaccessible hid from our eyes,*
> *Most blessed, most glorious, the Ancient of Days,*
> *Almighty, victorious, Thy great name we praise.*
>
> *Unresting, unhasting, and silent as light,*
> *Nor wanting, nor wasting, Thou rulest in might.*
> *Thy justice like mountains high soaring above*
> *Thy clouds which are fountains of goodness and love.*
>
> *To all, life Thou givest, to both great and small;*
> *In all life Thou livest, the true life of all.*
> *We blossom and flourish as leaves on the tree,*
> *And wither and perish, but naught changeth Thee.*
>
> *Great Father of glory, pure Father of light,*
> *Thine angels adore Thee, all veiling their sight.*
> *All praise we would render: O help us to see*
> *'Tis only the splendor of light hideth Thee.*[2]

I discovered that the hymn was based on 1 Timothy 1:17: "Now to the King eternal, immortal, invisible, to God who alone is wise, be honor and glory forever and ever. Amen."

We worship a God we cannot see. In the same way that we cannot look directly at the sun without destroying our eyesight, we cannot view God in our present bodies. Even the angels cover their faces in God's presence as they cry, "Holy, holy, holy is the LORD of hosts; the whole earth is full of His glory!" (Isaiah 6:3). One day we will be able to see his Son face to face, but not today.

At least now I knew how to be one who "dwelleth." The life of Jesus Christ is formed in us as naturally as springs flow, the dawn arrives, and the sunset beckons the night sky. His touch was mine for the asking. And I could say without a doubt, "You are my hiding place from every storm of life" (Psalm 32:7, TLB).

While I waited for more letters from Kathleen, peace permeated my soul.

I was at rest in the nest.

ELEVEN

Desert

LONDON
1911

*[Jesus said,] "Let not your heart be troubled; you
believe in God, believe also in Me."* JOHN 14:1

"You're kidding, right, Kathleen? You mean the first student at
the Bible Training College actually disappeared in the middle
of the night? How did that happen?" As usual, I was up in the
wee hours of the morning in order to talk to Kathleen during
the day, her time. (I didn't mind, though. What she talked
about was worth the effort. I learned from her that "one
should get up first and then think about it afterward.")

"Well," she interjected, "it wasn't quite that dramatic."

It seems that even though a great deal of preparation had
been undertaken for Mr. A. B. (the first student), including
his interview with the principal (Oswald Chambers), and
although a fluffy pillow along with freshly laundered sheets
had been placed carefully on a single bed in a little room

overlooking Clapham Common, the student disappeared nonetheless.

I had first wondered, *What was Clapham Common?* one fine day while walking the dog. The words had stuck in my mind since Kathleen had mentioned the Bible Training College was located near there.

Since I wasn't familiar with London, I had no idea what Clapham Common was, and I didn't want to run the telephone bill too high by taking the time to ask Kathleen.

I had managed to locate it on the map, however, and after polling a few people, I even found photographs. Clapham Common was a huge park, about two hundred acres of well-maintained grassland. It sported three ponds, stocked with fish. Many fine homes were built around the park, and from inside the Bible Training College, the students could view the peaceful scene.

God had provided above all expectations for the site, and the building was of the finest decor. The B.T.C. boasted high ceilings complete with artistic paintings, chandeliers, imitation marble pillars, an immense drawing room (which became the lecture hall), and enough room to house about two dozen students.

Over the time period of our letters and telephone conversations, Kathleen enlightened me as to how the Bible Training College came to be.

Kathleen explained that the League of Prayer, of which Oswald was a leading figure, felt the necessity of providing a training college for Christian service.

The idea would be to offer students solid Bible teaching where the whole Bible was considered to be both inspired and authoritative as God's Word. Also provided would be daily lessons in holiness, practical faith, and soul winning.

Since Oswald had experienced this type of training at Dunoon, he was the first choice to head up the school, and Biddy—his wife, his helpmeet—would be a perfect addition.

Members of the League of Prayer planned, prayed, and expected God to answer, as promised in Scripture: "If any of you lack wisdom, let him ask of God, that giveth to all men liberally, and upbraideth not; and it shall be given him. But let him ask in faith, nothing wavering. For he that wavereth is like a wave of the sea driven with the wind and tossed" (James 1:5-6, KJV). They believed God would provide the right leadership.

And so it was that a stately, large accommodation was found in a fashionable part of South London, with a view overlooking Clapham Common. The magnificent building was in excellent repair. Huge gilt mirrors hung over both mantelpieces. Paneled walls gave an air of cozy comfort.

The ornate mirrors were a constant reminder to the students that "we all, with unveiled face, beholding as in a mirror the glory of the Lord, are being transformed into the same image from glory to glory, just as by the Spirit of the Lord" (2 Corinthians 3:18).

Just like the early Christians after Pentecost, these believers were empowered by the Holy Spirit. They were in one accord and "all that believed were together, and had all things common" (Acts 2:44, KJV). Friends of the undertaking gave time and money, all the while feeling that this was God's will. And so God provided.

Furniture suitable for the college included straight-backed wooden chairs for the lecture hall and a large dining table for informal meals (where much of the actual teaching and discussing of Scripture occurred).

Single beds for the students' sleeping quarters and other

donations of small necessities from friends arrived each day to make it feel like home.

When the students arrived for meals, an elegant table-cloth covered the table. There were proper place settings, along with sparkling-clean goblets. Vases of fresh flowers completed the fine arrangements.

Biddy and Oswald always thanked God for his provision.

Biddy, an excellent housekeeper, enjoyed the preparations, and meals were served "as unto the Lord." She warmly welcomed missionaries and other visitors, as well as the students, to the Bible Training College, which was also home to Biddy and Oswald Chambers.

Biddy had the gift of hospitality and was a first-class hostess, and she and Oswald were always open to those who needed rest and recuperation, both physically and spiritually. Being rightly related to Jesus Christ filtered through to every aspect of life at the Bible Training College.

But back to the story of the missing student.

"So, Kathleen," I continued, during that phone call, "what exactly *did* happen to the student? And weren't Biddy and Oswald just a bit discouraged? After all, to have gone to all that work, and the student had been cleared and everything, and his bed was even made, and breakfast would be ready the next morning."

"As I said," Kathleen replied, "it wasn't that dramatic."

"Well, what did happen?" Suddenly I recalled a verse from the Bible: "Even fools are thought wise when they keep silent; with their mouths shut, they seem intelligent" (Proverbs 17:28, NLT). I wondered when I would ever learn to let Kathleen tell the story *her* way. I decided to try putting my hand over my mouth.

Kathleen continued, "My mother told me that the first student registered and accepted, a Mr. A. B., was welcomed at the college by my father himself, about ten in the evening. During the night, however, Mr. A. B. decided the college was not for him, and so he departed with all his baggage and was never seen or heard from after that time.

"And no, to answer your question," Kathleen went on, "my mother and father were not discouraged at the loss of their first student. Everything was an opportunity to do the next thing for God and Christ's Kingdom."

In the dim recesses of my brain, I remembered that in a medieval place of worship somewhere in England (or it might have been Scotland) was a wall hanging that said, "Doe The Next Thinge." I made a mental note to find that church someday.

> **M**y mother and father were not discouraged. Everything was an opportunity to do the next thing for God and Christ's Kingdom.
>
> —Kathleen Chambers

Quickly, I wrote on my notepad, "Find *Doe* and ask Kathleen."

In the meantime, Kathleen gave further details. "The Bible Training College, where I was later born, opened January 12, 1911. All the different branches of the church were represented, and there was no division among social classes."

I realized, in listening to Kathleen while remembering to

keep my mouth closed, that the entire venture was ordained by God, provided for by God, and empowered by his Holy Spirit through faithful believers in Jesus Christ.

The amazing thing to me about Kathleen's faith in Jesus Christ was that it seemed so very natural to her. Prayer was not a separate time away from life. Praying—"talking to the Almighty"—was her get-up-and-go, her strength. And that, she explained, was the atmosphere of the Bible Training College.

In the beginning, when God created the earth, he also gave us the ability to hear and obey him. Prayer, "the ministry of the interior" as Oswald called it, overcomes all obstacles because of our assurance of God's great love for us.

Kathleen was teaching me by her living example that a large part of believing was having faith in God's goodness and living in his love. She never doubted God's love for her and for humanity.

The Bible Training College was more than a beautiful mansion; it was a haven pointing the way to the heavenlies where Jesus has gone to prepare a place for each of us who belong to him.

The students learned that to love Jesus Christ above all else was to be identified with him: "I have been crucified with Christ; it is no longer I who live, but Christ lives in me; and the life which I now live in the flesh I live by faith in the Son of God, who loved me and gave Himself for me" (Galatians 2:20).

They discovered the faith that moves mountains because they understood they had been freely given the same faith in God demonstrated by Jesus as he willingly gave his life on the cross.

The atmosphere of the Bible Training College was charged with the Holy Spirit. Kathleen continually showed me that to trust God means to live out one's faith in the power of that same Spirit and that the only way to know God is to obey Jesus Christ, not merely because he demands it but because we love him:

> *Jesus said to [Thomas], "I am the way, the truth, and the life. No one comes to the Father except through Me. If you had known Me, you would have known My Father also; and from now on you know Him and have seen Him."*
>
> *Philip said to Him, "Lord, show us the Father, and it is sufficient for us."*
>
> *Jesus said to him, "Have I been with you so long, and yet you have not known Me, Philip? He who has seen Me has seen the Father; so how can you say, 'Show us the Father'? Do you not believe that I am in the Father, and the Father in Me? The words that I speak to you I do not speak on My own authority; but the Father who dwells in Me does the works. Believe Me that I am in the Father and the Father in Me, or else believe Me for the sake of the works themselves.*
>
> *"Most assuredly, I say to you, he who believes in Me, the works that I do he will do also; and greater works than these he will do, because I go to My Father.*
>
> *"And whatever you ask in My name, that I will do, that the Father may be glorified in the Son. If you ask anything in My name, I will do it.*
>
> *"If you love Me, keep My commandments. And I will pray the Father, and He will give you another Helper, that He may abide with you forever—the Spirit*

*of truth, whom the world cannot receive, because it
neither sees Him nor knows Him; but you know Him,
for He dwells with you and will be in you. I will not
leave you orphans; I will come to you.*

*"A little while longer and the world will see Me no
more, but you will see Me. Because I live, you will live
also. At that day you will know that I am in My Father,
and you in Me, and I in you."* JOHN 14:6-20

If students at the Bible Training College expressed fear about
following God's plan by faith and not by sight, they were
met with the words, "If thou canst!" This was in reference to
Mark 9:23, where Jesus said to the father of a sick child, "If
thou canst believe, all things are possible" (KJV).

The word *can't* wasn't in the B.T.C. vocabulary.

The Bible Training College provided an environment
where faith was a daily practice. Doubt and concern were to
have no place there.

John Wesley once said, "I would no more fret and worry
than I could curse and swear."

Oswald Chambers often said, "I refuse to worry."

Kathleen showed me that for a child of God concern
and anxiety are disobedience. Therefore, no matter what the
circumstances, we are to believe God's Word. Even though the
first student departed in the middle of the night, the college
soon became a well-known and highly respected institution.

On February 8, 1912, the college celebrated its first
anniversary. Although it was often thought that the college
should have failed financially (there was sometimes only
enough money to last a week), God always provided. And
Biddy managed to feed the students nutritious meals by
trusting God.

"Domestic students" soon arrived, greatly assisting Biddy in the necessary daily tasks. These students did a great deal of the cooking and the cleaning while at the same time sustaining high marks in their studies.

Students enthusiastically attended the Bible classes, where each week they studied an entire chapter, outlining it on a blackboard and identifying the main theme. That wasn't all. The students were to apply the lessons in their daily lives.

The students learned that "spiritual success" was a snare and that the life hidden with Christ in God was a result of obeying Jesus Christ out of love and maintaining a right relationship to him.

Students accepted the fact that one life "wholly yielded to God" was worth far more to God than many lives only "awakened."

It was this same belief that carried Biddy Chambers through the rest of her life and into eternity with Christ.

Prayer was often offered by all, asking that God would impart his Holy Spirit throughout the entire house, the result of which was that the students became saturated in God's love in the same way that seeds need to "soak" to germinate.

The students and Mr. and Mrs. Chambers believed and practiced Matthew 6:33: "Seek ye first the kingdom of God, and his righteousness; and all these things shall be added unto you" (KJV).

Students saw Oswald and Biddy living the Sermon on the Mount. The emphasis was never on self. The teaching was not denominational; it was biblical. Viewpoints were never forced; they were simply offered for consideration.

Early in the morning, a bell sounded, strains of music

filled the air, and the students would file into the lecture hall. Once they had assembled, Oswald Chambers would offer a short prayer. Then he lectured for about an hour while the students took notes.

He taught them to give all they had and to be yielded entirely to the Holy Spirit, and then to expect to receive everything necessary from God.

The students at B.T.C. understood and accepted that suffering, loss, and sorrow would come to the men and women who gave their all for God, but they eagerly plunged into the life of faith.

Trust in God was the only key that would unlock the door of the heart and fling it wide open for him to use as he pleased. The students learned to know Christ, who said, "Take My yoke upon you and learn from Me . . . and you will find rest for your souls" (Matthew 11:29).

They learned that finite creatures cannot understand an infinite God but that trust in his love was sufficient.

This time of close harmony and fellowship with one another as believers in Jesus Christ would be needed to carry them forward as world events rose to a crisis. Little did they know they would be scattered around the globe.

In 1913, Kathleen was born and entered into the life of the college as a baby much loved and cherished by all of the students. In that same year, a peace conference in London broke down over a Turkish refusal to yield Adrianople, the capital city of one of the administrative regions of the Ottoman Empire.

Mohandas Gandhi led more than two thousand Indians in defiance of a law and was jailed. A protest demonstration erupted, and police fired into the crowd, killing several of Gandhi's supporters and injuring many others who were present.

In that same year in Germany, a commercial ammonia plant began production at Ludwigshafen am Rhein. The ammonia would be used to make explosives.

It was anything but peaceful outside the walls of the Bible Training College.

Inside, however, the peaceful environment of the lecture hall prevailed as students listened and learned to live for the Lord Jesus Christ and to allow him full sway in all things.

Prayer charged the Bible Training College with God's presence. In fact, Kathleen told me about the time Oswald had given away their last half crown, and he asked his wife what she thought about that. Biddy, his excellent wife, simply replied they would have to trust God for another.

Oswald had given away their last half crown, and he asked his wife what she thought about that. Biddy, his excellent wife, simply replied they would have to trust God for another.

They did, and he supplied.

Hebrews 13:7 offers the instruction to "remember your leaders who taught you the word of God. Think of all the good that has come from their lives, and follow the example of their faith" (NLT). Oswald and Biddy Chambers were examples to follow in trust and obedience to Jesus Christ.

Circumstances around the world were changing. The

world teetered on the edge of a terrible great war. Very soon, increasing conflict among nations and powers would cause the bottom of order to fall out.

Like a tide of fast-flowing lava, the eruption of violence would impact unsuspecting nations.

Seclusion was not an option for the believers.

The lessons of faith they had learned would soon be put to the test.

TWELVE

𝒱alley

LONDON
1915

> *It came to pass, when the time had come for [Jesus]*
> *to be received up, that He steadfastly set His face to*
> *go to Jerusalem.*   LUKE 9:51

As the First World War gradually engulfed most of the globe, the calamity resulted in the closure of the Bible Training College for the duration of the war. And in October 1915, Oswald Chambers strode resolutely forward as he approached the ramp of the ship that would carry him far away from England; the Bible Training College; his faithful students; his dear wife, Biddy; and his "Little Flower of God," Kathleen.

Oswald's destination was the Zeitoun Training Base, located in Egypt. His objective was to minister to the troops stationed there. Oswald was an experienced traveler, but this was the first time his work required him to leave his young wife and tiny daughter behind.

As he neared the ship, Oswald carried his little daughter on his right side while he hefted his heavy luggage on the left.

Even though the time of Oswald's departure was at hand, and even though Biddy would not be going with him, she smiled cheerfully as she walked along at his side.

Then, it was time for him to leave.

Little Kathleen giggled with glee when Oswald lowered his baggage to the ground in order to free both hands to lift her high above his head before swinging her down and hugging her close to his heart.

He handed Kathleen to Biddy.

Then he was gone.

Biddy looked forward to seeing her husband again in December of that same year, when she hoped to join him in that faraway place. But in doing so she would be leaving home and all that she knew and transferring a tiny young girl to the desert sands of Egypt.

During the next few weeks, while making the necessary arrangements and carefully packing for herself and her daughter, she reflected on the world crisis causing her to relocate to a military training camp near Cairo, Egypt, more than two thousand miles from her family and friends.

While carefully pressing ribbons and bows needed for Kathleen's hair, Biddy remembered the last few days of the Bible Training College.

Oswald had been a tower of strength to all because he relied totally on Jesus Christ for everything, from the smallest detail to the impending global war that had forced the college to close.

Biddy watched little Kathleen as she busily "helped" her to move things and pack and clean.

What would health and sanitation be like in Egypt? She

brushed the thought aside. "I will trust God," she said out loud. "He never fails us."

She thought about the final words spoken when the Bible Training College finally closed on July 14, 1915, and how the message was one of hope in the Lord Jesus Christ: "Let not your heart be troubled; you believe in God, believe also in Me" (John 14:1).

As the students, staff, Biddy, and Kathleen listened intently, they were reminded that with God there would be no real good-bye because the love of Jesus Christ was sealed in their hearts by the Holy Spirit.

Biddy would be leaving home and all that she knew and transferring a tiny young girl to the desert sands of Egypt.

Biddy and Oswald lived in the light of Luke 11:13: "If you then, being evil, know how to give good gifts to your children, how much more will your heavenly Father give the Holy Spirit to those who ask Him!"

"Oswald will be taking the Lord Jesus Christ to the men," Biddy announced. She paused in her packing long enough to give Kathleen a quick hug. "And we must be ready!"

Little Kathleen held up her doll to her mother. "For trip!"

"Yes, for the journey," Biddy replied. "And your ribbons will be nicely prepared too."

Kathleen, living the simple life of a child, smiled happily and then found a fly to chase.

It was a year earlier, in 1914, when World War I began in Europe. It was May 1915 when Oswald felt God's call to offer spiritual first aid to the troops. He based his decision on 2 Timothy 4:6: "I am now ready to be offered, and the time of my departure is at hand" (KJV).

Then, since he was a thoughtful son, he wrote to his parents, informing them of his decision.

Oswald was confident that Biddy would stand beside him, no matter the cost. He thought his destination might be a Y.M.C.A. hut. In May 1915, he wasn't certain of all the details, but he knew the One who did know, and that was all that mattered. He knew the details would fall into place.

Biddy felt privileged to be Oswald's wife. He lived the Bible and walked the way Jesus walked. Biddy knew God would engineer the circumstances and that Oswald would always follow him.

Biddy paused while folding little Kathleen's clothes. She realized Egypt might be dreadful. She had been advised by all who had been to the desert sands of Egypt that she would have to live underground because no one could stand the heat of the day and stay alive without shelter. Some "helpful" acquaintances even went so far as to suggest the attempt would be impossible and would probably fail.

She thought for a moment about why Oswald was in Egypt and not some other part of the world. The British had colonized Egypt as a source of revenue, so Great Britain had important financial interests there. Egypt, on the other hand, depended on Britain to export its raw cotton. Egypt had also come to rely on Britain for manufactured goods. So when World War I broke out and began to escalate,

Egypt was brought formally into the British Empire as a protectorate.

The Suez Canal was a vital lifeline for Britain. It was the crucial shortcut between India and Europe. The Canal and the Abadan oil pipeline had to be guarded at all costs.

Because of the broad scope of the war and Britain's involvement, troops from various countries were represented. Troops defending the Suez Canal could be reinforced quickly by the training camps near Cairo.

Most of the men accepted into the British army in August 1914 were sent first to Egypt, not Europe, to meet the threat posed to British interests by the Ottoman Empire in the Middle East and the Suez Canal.

In 1915, when Oswald Chambers sailed to Zeitoun, Egypt, just seven miles from Cairo, to join the staff of the Y.M.C.A., he would be part of the Mediterranean Expeditionary Force at the Zeitoun Training Base. The base was a vast military camp located in the open desert. It held Australian and New Zealand forces, but English and Scottish troops were represented as well. The young soldiers slept in tents and huts. There were lines of horses, ambulances, and wagons, all surrounded by the vast expanse of desert. The conditions of the camp were horrendous. The sun shone relentlessly. Insects were everywhere.

The most tormenting pests, flies and mosquitoes, covered the camp like low-flying clouds. The men suffered constantly from the merciless bites and required fly whisks to keep the bugs out of their eyes and ears.

Lack of anything to do made the monotonous long days even more trying. Word from home seldom arrived, and the nerves of the young men wore thin as they faced the heat, the blowing sand, the insects, the sparse meals, and the constant fact that this day might be their last day on earth. If a soldier became ill, he had to be sent to Cairo, traveling through intense heat. If a young man survived, he would be sent to another camp in Cairo or to Alexandria to recuperate. Going home was not an option.

Oswald would serve as the soldiers' chaplain, friend, and counselor. Oswald and Biddy wanted to comfort the soldiers and share the gospel. They wanted to prepare the way for the young men, many of them still in their teens, to face eternity. They planned to share the way Home.

The Y.M.C.A. hut, Biddy and Kathleen's new dwelling, would be made of matting nailed to wooden supports. Desert sand would provide the floor surface.

The hut would be their protection from the khamsin, a hot, driving windstorm. Similar to the sirocco, the Mediterranean wind coming from the Sahara Desert could reach hurricane speeds. The violent dust storms might last one day or many, no one knew.

Those living in such dry and dusty conditions might suffer health problems as a result, not to mention the fact that the powerful winds could easily destroy necessary military machines and vehicles.

In London, as Biddy Chambers washed, ironed, and prepared tablecloths for the tea she would provide for the men, she could only imagine what the dust would do to her tables and chairs.

She had been told that the men usually ate their dreary meals outside around a campfire, served from an outdoor kitchen.

Biddy was grateful to God that later she would have several of the Bible Training College students coming from London to help her. Because of the dangers involved, they were uncertain for a time if any women at all would be allowed to visit, let alone stay, at a military base of operations. The fact that permits had been granted for these English ladies to travel to a military training camp was again proof that God was paving the way.

Also of comfort to Biddy Chambers was the fact that Mary Riley, a B.T.C. student, would travel with her and Kathleen to Zeitoun.

"Mama?" Little Kathleen appeared.

"My Little Flower of God!" Biddy smiled and scooped her toddler into her arms. "I'll bet you are hungry."

"Yes, Mama," Kathleen replied. "I couldn't get any flies!"

"That's all right, darling," Biddy replied, setting her down on her feet. "Flies are very fast."

Once toddler Kathleen was fed and down for her afternoon nap, Biddy returned to her thoughts and her packing.

After sorting through more items to take to Egypt, Biddy sank down momentarily on a footstool. Her spirits rose, however, when she remembered the words of Jesus: "Why take ye thought for raiment? Consider the lilies of the field, how they grow; they toil not, neither do they spin" (Matthew 6:28, KJV).

She prayed silently, *Aboveground or underground, it is all the same to thee.*

She opened her Bible for reassurance and grabbed her handy notebook. God's Word never failed. She knew that Oswald did not give way to moods of depression, so she would go to the source of peace and comfort.

Slowly, carefully, she read the following passages:

> *Thou wilt keep him in perfect peace, whose mind is stayed on thee: because he trusteth in thee.*
>
> ISAIAH 26:3 (KJV)

Thus saith the LORD that created thee, O Jacob, and he that formed thee, O Israel, Fear not: for I have redeemed thee, I have called thee by thy name; thou art mine.

When thou passest through the waters, I will be with thee; and through the rivers, they shall not overflow thee: when thou walkest through the fire, thou shalt not be burned; neither shall the flame kindle upon thee.

For I am the LORD thy God, the Holy One of Israel, thy Saviour: I gave Egypt for thy ransom, Ethiopia and Seba for thee.

Since thou wast precious in my sight, thou hast been honourable, and I have loved thee: therefore will I give men for thee, and people for thy life.

Fear not: for I am with thee: I will bring thy seed from the east, and gather thee from the west; I will say to the north, Give up; and to the south, Keep not back: bring my sons from far, and my daughters from the ends of the earth; even every one that is called by my name: for I have created him for my glory, I have formed him; yea, I have made him.

Bring forth the blind people that have eyes, and the deaf that have ears.

Let all the nations be gathered together, and let the people be assembled: who among them can declare this, and shew us former things? let them bring forth their witnesses, that they may be justified: or let them hear, and say, It is truth.

Ye are my witnesses, saith the LORD, and my servant whom I have chosen: that ye may know and believe me, and understand that I am he: before me there was no God formed, neither shall there be after me.

*I, even I, am the LORD; and beside me there is no
saviour. I have declared, and have saved, and I have
shewed, when there was no strange god among you:
therefore ye are my witnesses, saith the LORD, that
I am God.*

*Yea, before the day was I am he; and there is none
that can deliver out of my hand: I will work, and who
shall let it?*

*Thus saith the LORD, your redeemer, the Holy One
of Israel; For your sake I have sent to Babylon, and
have brought down all their nobles, and the Chaldeans,
whose cry is in the ships. I am the LORD, your Holy
One, the creator of Israel, your King.*

*Thus saith the LORD, which maketh a way in the
sea, and a path in the mighty waters. . . .*

*Remember ye not the former things, neither consider
the things of old. Behold, I will do a new thing; now it
shall spring forth; shall ye not know it?*

*I will even make a way in the wilderness, and rivers
in the desert. The beast of the field shall honour me,
the dragons and the owls: because I give waters in the
wilderness, and rivers in the desert, to give drink to my
people, my chosen. This people have I formed for myself;
they shall shew forth my praise.*   ISAIAH 43:1-21 (KJV)

Reverently, Biddy closed her Bible and held it close to her
heart for a moment. Then she noted the Scripture references
in her notebook. "Oswald will enjoy these," she said softly.

She worked and packed until it was time to prepare her
daughter's evening meal.

Once the little one was bathed and safely asleep for the
night, Biddy returned to her tasks. In the same way the

virtuous wives of old carried on without complaint, Biddy was faithful: "Strength and honor are her clothing; she shall rejoice in time to come" (Proverbs 31:25).

Mrs. Oswald Chambers did not worry. She honored her husband even when she was not with him. She prayed.

Biddy studied God's Word: "Be anxious for nothing, but in everything by prayer and supplication, with thanksgiving, let your requests be made known to God" (Philippians 4:6), and she obeyed.

Just before she tucked herself into bed for the night, she sang her favorite hymn:

> *Abide with me; fast falls the eventide;*
> *The darkness deepens; Lord with me abide.*
> *When other helpers fail and comforts flee,*
> *Help of the helpless, O abide with me.*
>
> *Swift to its close ebbs out life's little day;*
> *Earth's joys grow dim; its glories pass away;*
> *Change and decay in all around I see;*
> *O Thou who changest not, abide with me.*
>
> *Not a brief glance I beg, a passing word;*
> *But as Thou dwell'st with Thy disciples, Lord,*
> *Familiar, condescending, patient, free.*
> *Come not to sojourn, but abide with me.*
>
> *Come not in terrors, as the King of kings,*
> *But kind and good, with healing in Thy wings,*
> *Tears for all woes, a heart for every plea—*
> *Come, Friend of sinners, and thus bide with me.*
>
> *I need Thy presence every passing hour.*
> *What but Thy grace can foil the tempter's power?*

Who, like Thyself, my guide and stay can be?
Through cloud and sunshine, Lord, abide with me.

I fear no foe, with Thee at hand to bless;
Ills have no weight, and tears no bitterness.
Where is death's sting? Where, grave, thy victory?
I triumph still, if Thou abide with me.

Hold Thou Thy cross before my closing eyes;
Shine through the gloom and point me to the skies.
Heaven's morning breaks, and earth's vain shadows flee;
In life, in death, O Lord, abide with me.[1]

Soon Biddy Chambers, like her little daughter, was fast asleep. The faraway land of Egypt would hold no terror for her because she rested in the truth of Scripture: "Springs will burst forth in the wilderness, and streams in the desert" (Isaiah 35:6, TLB).

Biddy, like a child at rest, was secure in God's love, and the God of peace held Biddy and her child close to himself.

THIRTEEN

*B*eginning

LONDON/BRITISH COLUMBIA
1917

> *When they walk through the Valley of Weeping,*
> *it will become a place of refreshing springs. The*
> *autumn rains will clothe it with blessings.*

PSALM 84:6, NLT

It was three in the morning my time, in North America, in the year of our Lord 1995. I drummed my fingers on my desk, eagerly waiting for Kathleen Chambers to answer the phone. I had an important question to ask her.

"Four rings," I muttered to myself. "She usually answers by the second ring—Kathleen! You are there after all." I couldn't keep from elevating my tone.

"Yes," she answered, sounding somewhat bewildered, "shouldn't I be?"

"Sorry about that. I just wanted to talk to you because I have come across something, and I would like to have your opinion about it. I guess patience isn't one of my virtues."

"It should be—" she began to remark, gently.

"Anyway," I interrupted, "I've been thinking about our discussion last week, about the lilies of the field and the stars in the sky, and how God loves us more than we can imagine."

"Yes," she replied. "I'm smiling."

"Okay, good, because this could take a few minutes."

"It usually does." She chuckled good-naturedly.

"Here goes. . . . In Matthew 6:28, in the King James Version, Jesus says, 'Why take ye thought for raiment? Consider the lilies of the field, how they grow; they toil not, neither do they spin.' That's the first thought."

I waited for her to reply. She didn't.

"The second idea is about the stars that shine in the heavens. Are you still there?"

"Yes. Go on. I am interested." Kathleen was always so kind.

"How did your mother look at that?"

I heard her take a breath, or sigh a little. "My mother felt that we should never worry about money because God would always provide. She felt that to be concerned that way, especially to talk of finances before others and to say it would cost too much to afford it (whatever the item was), would result in poverty of spirit because God would provide for us—just like the lilies of the field. Have you read the rest of the chapter?"

"Oh, okay. Hold on a moment."

Finding it quickly, I read aloud, "Yet I say unto you, That even Solomon in all his glory was not arrayed like one of these. Wherefore, if God so clothe the grass of the field, which to day is, and to morrow is cast into the oven, shall he not much more clothe you, O ye of little faith? Therefore take no thought, saying, What shall we eat? or, What shall we drink? or, Wherewithal shall we be clothed?" (Matthew 6:29-31, KJV). "So, how did your mother do that?"

Patiently Kathleen explained the "how" of it to me the way a mother instructs a small child. "My mother talked to God about money. He always provided, sometimes in surprising ways."

"That's it?" I had already known what her response would be, so I plunged ahead to the next subject without stopping to catch my breath. "So, how does a star act, exactly? I mean, it shines, right? So, our lives are supposed to shine the light of Jesus Christ in the world, right?"

"Slow down a bit, Ducks," Kathleen quickly interjected.

I always liked it when she used that term because it denoted affection. She had always called her mother "My Old Girl." I relaxed in my desk chair and waited for her words of wisdom.

"The lilies of the field show God's loving care for us. The stars, on the other hand, display the glory of God. They just are. When you see the stars at night, a great calm caresses your soul. This was especially true for my mother and father when they observed them in Egypt."

Then she explained, "My father believed that stars are serene, physically sound, true to themselves, and not concerned with fussy events. The Bible says it better than I can: 'The heavens declare the glory of God; and the firmament showeth his handywork.'"

"Oh, yes, I love that verse. Psalm 19:1 in the King James Version, right?"

"I think so," she patiently responded. "You see," Kathleen continued unwearyingly, "life in the desert was quiet and monotonous for the soldiers. The early mornings were a great blessing of peace for the day because the rising of the sun was full of color and the promise of God's provision, no matter what the day might bring.

"The stars at night reminded my mother and father of the timelessness of God, his infinite power and might. As the stars began to sprinkle light across the desert sky, the busyness, the worrying, and the doing-goodness took their proper place of unimportance. God seemed very close to them in the desert. God would always be there. He *is,* and *was,* and always *will be.*"

"Do you remember the desert, Kathleen?"

"Not really, but my mother told me so much about it that it is very real in my memory."

Listening to Kathleen had brought quiet to my soul, and I realized that many things that seem very important in modern everyday life are really of no consequence. I realized that so much of the controversy that confuses people really comes from our own doing. "Or undoing," I remarked to Cookie, my little dog, who slept quietly in his bed.

Sitting in my rocking chair by the picture window in the quiet just before dawn, I read, "The wisdom of this world is foolishness to God. As the Scriptures say, 'He traps the wise in the snare of their own cleverness'" (1 Corinthians 3:19, NLT).

Since it was almost daylight, I decided to take Cookie outside with me to watch the quiet of the stars give way to the splendor of the sun. I could only imagine what it must have been like in the desert. A great calm soothed my spirit. I was not anxious, or afraid, or worried.

All at once, Cookie started barking at the top of his lungs.

Suddenly alert, I grabbed my little dog and hurried inside. "You know, Cookie, we do have bears around this neighborhood!" Then, I laughed at my lack of faith. God was bigger than a bear. When would I realize it?

Kathleen said that to abide in God meant to think about him at least one minute out of every hour.

Later, as I began my daily chores, I reflected on God's Word. I hoped I could learn to put that into practice. *No,* I reasoned, *God can make it a reality.* I copied down the verses Kathleen and I had discussed and put them on the door of my refrigerator, resolving to commit them to memory:

> *Why worry about your clothing? Look at the lilies of the field and how they grow. They don't work or make their clothing, yet Solomon in all his glory was not dressed as beautifully as they are. And if God cares so wonderfully for wildflowers that are here today and thrown into the fire tomorrow, he will certainly care for you. Why do you have so little faith?*
>
> *So don't worry about these things, saying, "What will we eat? What will we drink? What will we wear?" These things dominate the thoughts of unbelievers, but your heavenly Father already knows all your needs. Seek the Kingdom of God above all else, and live righteously, and he will give you everything you need.*
>
> *So don't worry about tomorrow, for tomorrow will bring its own worries. Today's trouble is enough for today.* MATTHEW 6:28-34 (NLT)

Two days later I was on the phone again to Kathleen. "You know, Kathleen, you taught me so much the other day that I've been thinking."

"You usually are," she chuckled with good humor. "What about?"

"Grapes."

"Grapes?"

"Yes, grapes. I've been thinking about what it must be like to be a grape."

"Let me sit down first."

"Okay. Here goes . . . Your mother and father taught that we are to be like broken bread and poured-out wine for the nourishment of others."

"Yes."

"So, I've been thinking about what it must be like to be a grape."

"Be a *grape.*" Kathleen slowly repeated my words.

"Yes. I've been doing some research on this and have asked a few knowledgeable people who grow grapes, and I've made an outline."

"Yes."

"First, a tiny bud appears on the vine and gets pushed around a bit by the leaves. But I've been told that the vine is very strong and capable of feeding and housing the grapes, so that part is okay.

"Then the little bud gets wind and rain on its face.

"After that, the grape grower maybe dumps insect stuff around the vine, and maybe some smelly fertilizer on the ground. That has to be a bit of a shock. Anyway, after that, the bud hears sounds of shears and weed pulling and other scary things."

I stopped long enough to ascertain that Kathleen was still breathing at the other end of the phone line before I continued. She was.

"Then, glory hallelujah, the little bud turns into a grape, and all is well! Are you following this, Kathleen?"

"Yes, I'm still here."

"Good, because here comes the part that isn't so good. The little grape ripens and loves the air and the sunshine and the environment, but then the grape grower comes and yanks it from its home; tosses it, along with other grapes, into a basket; and takes it away from all that is familiar. That's devastating enough, but after the little grape gets washed (nearly drowned), it is going to die by getting crushed!"

Kathleen stayed on the other end of the phone, and she didn't even remind me how expensive the call was for me.

"Finally, Kathleen, here comes the good news, and that's why I called."

"Why?"

"Because guess where the grape winds up?"

"Where?"

"At the Lord's Table! Isn't that wonderful? So, I'm figuring that to be a grape means I will probably have to suffer a bit, get squished and all, in order to become wine, but I will wind up at the Lord's Table!"

"And the lesson is?"

"That's what I wanted to run past you, Kathleen. It seems to me that a grape has no choice, but we can, if we will, choose to be a little grape in God's tender care. Therefore, in our lives, like the grape, we will need to be used of God to nourish others, but it might cost us pain and sorrow in the meantime."

"Go on—this is interesting," Kathleen interjected.

"The whole point is that God doesn't force us to be a grape; that is, to choose to love and serve him just as Jesus did. But if we do yield our lives to him, we will be changed into his glory, just like Jesus."

"Your question is . . ."

"So, doesn't that mean that because your father and mother lived like grapes, and now you live like one, glory will be the result, not only for you personally but for all who come in contact with grapes? I even found a Scripture verse (1 Peter 5:10, NLT) to support my theory: 'In his kindness God called you to share in his eternal glory by means of Christ Jesus. So after you have suffered a little while, he will restore, support, and strengthen you, and he will place you on a firm foundation.'"

Just then, Kathleen's dog, Lady, needed to go outside, and of course, the call of nature couldn't wait. Anyway, I knew we would talk again soon.

The next day while doing some research, I came across a hymn that Kathleen had referenced at the close of our last conversation. It described the serene sky and wonderful stars experienced by Oswald and Biddy Chambers.

> *Still, still with Thee, when purple morning breaketh,*
> *When the bird waketh, and the shadows flee;*
> *Fairer than morning, lovelier than daylight,*
> *Dawns the sweet consciousness, I am with Thee.*

> *Alone with Thee, amid the mystic shadows,*
> *The solemn hush of nature newly born;*
> *Alone with Thee in breathless adoration,*
> *In the calm dew and freshness of the morn.*

> *As in the dawning o'er the waveless ocean*
> *The image of the morning star doth rest,*
> *So in the stillness Thou beholdest only*
> *Thine image in the waters of my breast.*

> *Still, still with Thee, as to each newborn morning,*
> *A fresh and solemn splendor still is given,*
> *So does this blessed consciousness, awaking,*
> *Breathe each day nearness unto Thee and Heaven.*

When sinks the soul, subdued by toil, to slumber,
Its closing eye looks up to Thee in prayer;
Sweet the repose beneath the wings o'ershading,
But sweeter still to wake and find Thee there.

So shall it be at last, in that bright morning,
When the soul waketh and life's shadows flee;
Oh in that hour, fairer than daylight dawning,
Shall rise the glorious thought, I am with Thee.[1]

While waiting for my next call or letter from Kathleen,
I resolved to find out more about what Biddy Chambers
would have gone through in her "grape life." I felt she
was a role model for me and for other women today who
really do want to follow after Jesus Christ each day. Was it
easy? I knew it couldn't have been. How did she manage? I
wondered as I wandered through pages of material.

My research, plus the information Kathleen had sent to
me previously, helped me to better understand the conditions of life waiting for Biddy Chambers in the desert.

Even though she had been advised that life in Egypt
would seem close to mere survival, she was unprepared for the
suffocating heat, the relentless wind, and the blowing sand.
When it did rain, it poured, drenching beds and tables and
chairs and depositing an accumulation of sand that stuck like
molasses to everything. The desert was a land of extremes.

It was December 1915 when Mrs. Oswald Chambers and
little Kathleen arrived in Egypt. They were accompanied by
Mary Riley, who had been with them at the Bible Training
College before it closed for the duration of the war. Zeitoun,
the training camp, was about seven miles from Cairo.

In my mind's eye, I could see Biddy's first encounter with World War I. What Biddy saw was a military camp in a vast expanse of open desert. The rows of tents stretching out before her seemed unending. Open campfires blazed in the hot sun. The most striking feature of the landscape must have been the soldiers waiting to be sent to the lines.

No young man should look like this, Biddy thought as she walked about the camp with Oswald. Soldiers huddled together in clumps, gathered around the open fires, or sat on the sand. Their faces showed the strain of war, making them look much older than their years. Their sunken cheeks told the tale of poor meals and little sleep.

By our standards, a field ambulance (jokingly referred to as a Rolls Royce), which served as the only way to a hospital, would have been enough to send many a modern woman searching for an immediate way back home. An ambulance looked a little like an early-style motorcar modified into a trucklike vehicle that sported spoke wheels and rubber tires. The sides were not covered, so the wind and sand whipped the passengers. The top, held up by wooden supports, resembled a canvas canopy. The journey to a hospital was extremely treacherous for patients.

"This is home," Oswald said quietly as he led her to a bungalow, the little house prepared for her arrival.

"How nice," she replied, with an encouraging smile for her husband.

Built inside the mission compound, the bungalow stood on a patch of sand. A great deal of love and prayer—as well as donations of materials and funds—had made this dwelling possible.

Most important, however, was the fact that the house was

built on the foundation of Jesus Christ, "a firm, tested, precious Cornerstone that is safe to build on" (Isaiah 28:16, TLB).

Kathleen was happy to be in her father's care. "See how happy our 'Little Flower of God' is to be here," Biddy offered.

Proud of his wife and content to carry Kathleen, Oswald Chambers showed Biddy the Y.M.C.A. hut.

The hut had a floor of desert sand. It was quite large, allowing room for a small platform at one end and rooms for the secretary at the other end.

Smiling all the while, Oswald gave his wife a tour of the sandy camp, on which the men and flies and mosquitoes and vehicles and tents and fires waited for the end of life or the end of the war.

Even though Biddy had been advised that life in Egypt would seem close to mere survival, she was unprepared for the suffocating heat, the relentless wind, and the blowing sand. When it did rain, it poured, drenching beds and tables and chairs and depositing an accumulation of sand that stuck like molasses to everything.

"All things are possible with God. Even if others don't believe it," he told her happily.

The first physical hurdle Biddy had to overcome was the sand. Tougher still to surmount would be the emotional trials of pain, weariness, disappointment, delay, and upset plans. She was ready, however, for she found strength in the joy of the Lord (see Nehemiah 8:10).

I probably would have said, "Get me the nearest camel, and get me out of here!"

Biddy, however, took things in stride. Nothing could match the cheerful way in which Miss Riley and Mrs. Oswald Chambers faced their new life. They did not complain. Confronting it all with courage, they settled right in and got to work. Biddy and her devoted husband believed in accepting the seemingly haphazard events of each day as coming from God: "We know that all things work together for good to them that love God, to them who are the called according to his purpose" (Romans 8:28, KJV).

Little Kathleen followed her mother's example, bringing delight to all she met. Kathleen's happy smile, however, seriously contrasted with the environment.

Biddy knew that soon others from the Bible Training College would arrive to help, once they had received the special military permits that would allow them to work among the troops.

Oswald was in charge of working with Australian and New Zealand forces, as well as with English and Scottish troops. Many of them would go directly to Gallipoli or other war fronts protecting the Suez Canal, and more than half would not return.

It was not an easy task, but Oswald marched steadily forward for his Lord, while the soldiers waited for their marching orders from headquarters. He knew that the yoke would be easy and the burden light as he believed, relied on God, and put his faith into practice. His hope, Jesus Christ, would never fail. The spiritual victory was certain.

Using the same methods he had found successful in his teaching at the Bible Training College, Oswald Chambers carefully instructed the men. Night after night he meticulously wrote outlines on a chalkboard. The men took notes.

He taught them that the reality of redemption in the

light of the Cross placed them on holy ground. Suffering opened spiritual doors to many who would otherwise not have bothered to seriously consider their existence.

To no one's surprise, the young soldiers eagerly anticipated and attended the lectures Oswald held in the Y.M.C.A. hut. There was no room for make-believe in life at the military camp. Suffering, sorrow, and the possibility of loss of life confronted all of those who waited to be sent to the lines. In the same way that the apostle Paul had preached to prisoners and Peter had shared the message of the Cross of Christ, Oswald counted nothing important unless it was of eternal consequence. These were souls in jeopardy. They all realized it.

Many who had held religious beliefs in their prior, civilized life found a personal relationship with Jesus in this place of constant monotony, uncertainty, and stress.

War had changed the world. Men were maimed beyond recovery and could never again resume their former lives of usefulness. Suffering opened the door to life. There could be no return to yesterday, but God, through the redemption of the Cross of Christ, could make a new and better future. Only the One who caused the lame to walk and the blind to see could give the men eternal life.

God's Word never returns void:

> *As the rain comes down, and the snow from heaven, and do not return there, but water the earth, and make it bring forth and bud, that it may give seed to the sower and bread to the eater, so shall My word be that goes forth from My mouth; it shall not return to Me void, but it shall accomplish what I please, and it shall prosper in the thing for which I sent it. For you shall go*

> *out with joy, and be led out with peace; the mountains*
> *and the hills shall break forth into singing before you,*
> *and all the trees of the field shall clap their hands.*
>
> ISAIAH 55:10-12

Patiently, I waited for Kathleen to pick up the telephone at her end. When she answered, I had another question for her.

"Kathleen, what was your mother doing while your father was preaching at the military camp?"

Silence.

"Kathleen, are you there?"

I waited for her cheery voice to reply. Nothing. Then I heard an operator say, "Hang up your call, and try again."

Sadly, I replaced the telephone receiver. "Sometimes that happens on a call across the ocean," I said out loud to encourage myself.

Little did I know that soon Kathleen wouldn't be there, ever again.

FOURTEEN

Jordan

ZEITOUN, EGYPT
1917

> *All creation is waiting eagerly for that future day*
> *when God will reveal who his children really are.*
>
> ROMANS 8:19, NLT

"Look, Mama! I'm riding my donkey!" Little four-year-old Kathleen sat proudly on the gift given to her by an Australian soldier at the military camp.

Biddy Chambers clapped her hands in delight while Oswald closely watched that the little animal behaved.

Kathleen wasn't concerned, however. She trusted her mother and father completely.

Animals were a large part of the home atmosphere created by Biddy Chambers. She cared for rabbits, cats (and the resulting kittens), stray tortoises, lizards, chameleons, doves, pigeons, and whatever else Kathleen brought home to her mother. Kathleen's "zoo" provided warmth to everyone.

Her happy childhood chatter crowded out the sound of distant guns.

Then, too, Biddy watched over and fed a great favorite of Oswald's named Patsy, a small black and tan collie with an excellent temperament. Each evening, after completing the duties for the day, Biddy and Oswald took their dog for a run in the desert. Their little house, called the Bungalow, was a light in a dark world, reminding the young men that home still meant something, life still mattered, and courage was confidence in a God who cared.

Because they were living daily in close association with Biddy, Oswald, Kathleen, and others from the Bible Training College, who were now present and working hard, many of the men discovered a personal relationship with Jesus Christ—even those who didn't know what they were seeking. The soldiers learned by example, as well as from Oswald's nightly teaching. Confronted by the faith of practical Christianity, they found their real home. Abiding peace in the midst of turmoil resulted.

Young military men from various parts of the world and very different backgrounds came to believe that dreadful circumstances could never conquer the power of almighty God.

A few days after my call to Kathleen failed, and after several conversations with the telephone companies, I tried again. "It is, after all, 1997," I groused, as I waited for the operator-assisted call to go through. My suggestion to the phone experts that we might be better off to return to drums, smoke signals, or string attached to tin cans had fallen on deaf ears.

Anxiously, I waited. Was Kathleen all right? Why hadn't

she answered my last call? Then I heard, "Person to person for Miss Kathleen Chambers. Is this Miss Chambers?"

"Yes," her wonderful, familiar voice immediately replied.

"Kathleen!"

"Yes."

"I've been so worried. How can I ever do this without you?"

"You really must learn to trust God, Ducks." Kathleen corrected my behavior, but her tone showed her love and affection for me. "He won't give you something to do and then leave you to wobble along without him. Something I like to remember is in Hebrews 13:5-6."

"Okay. Sorry about that. I'm better now, and I'll look up the reference as soon as we're off the phone today."

Kathleen's complete reliance on her heavenly Father was contagious.

"What I wanted to ask you, Kathleen, is this: What was your mother doing while your father was preaching at the military camp?"

"Oh, good question. Why don't I send you that in a letter? I am concerned about how long this will take on the telephone."

"Good idea! Thanks, Kathleen. I will wait patiently, and I'm smiling."

While waiting for mail from London, I looked up Hebrews 13:5-6: "He hath said, I will never leave thee, nor forsake thee. So that we may boldly say, The Lord is my helper, and I will not fear what man shall do unto me" (KJV).

Kathleen trusted God completely. I knew I had to learn how to follow her example. She trusted his Word. God would not lie.

Kathleen always kept her word, too, and it wasn't

long before I had an answer to my question. What I also wondered, though, was how Biddy Chambers could do all she did in sweltering heat and wearing long skirts. How did she keep the sand out of her eyes?

By 1917, Oswald had built a dugout underground that was used in the summer months and as a refuge on hot sunny days. I could only imagine how Biddy managed to keep that clean and tidy.

According to Kathleen, her mother was a trouper and didn't complain. Kathleen's information boggled my mind as I reviewed the way Biddy spent her time while her husband preached.

When the refreshment hut opened for the soldiers, Biddy saw to it that the men were greeted with tables covered in white tablecloths. A vase of flowers graced each table as a centerpiece.

As a hostess, Biddy Chambers was the quintessential woman outlined in Proverbs. Her grace and dignity created a sense of calm and tranquility for everyone, including Kathleen: "She watches over the ways of her household, and does not eat the bread of idleness" (Proverbs 31:27).

Kathleen's mother didn't just read her Bible each day, she lived it, and God carried her. "I was hungry and you gave Me food; I was thirsty and you gave Me drink; I was a stranger and you took Me in" (Matthew 25:35). A multitude of troubled soldiers sat down at tables standing on the sand and found the love of Jesus Christ in a free cup of tea.

Biddy Chambers was also a comforter. No matter how busy she was, she had time for soldiers and animals and children and her husband and, of course, her note taking.

Her experience in England as a stenographer came in handy as Biddy took down Oswald's messages, carefully recording them verbatim in her notebook. Did she know she was being given words for the world?

Sometimes Biddy Chambers led the morning service. She was a great inspiration to many as she opened God's Word. After giving a message on Romans 12:1, "I beseech you therefore, brethren, by the mercies of God, that you present your bodies a living sacrifice, holy, acceptable to God, which is your reasonable service," she quietly prepared the evening meal for everyone who appeared hungry. Most of all, Biddy Chambers was a lady. A lady, as defined by *Merriam-Webster,* is "a woman of refinement and gentle manners."[1]

A *multitude of troubled soldiers sat down at tables standing on the sand and found the love of Jesus Christ in a free cup of tea.*

On May 25, 1917, Biddy and Oswald celebrated their seventh wedding anniversary in the midst of war and suffering and pain. The lovely dawn reminded them of the shelter of God's love. God had transplanted them from England to Egypt, from a lovely home to a bungalow.

Kathleen told me that her mother had quoted her father to her, saying, "Where God leads, we follow, and a joy it is, too."

Jesus calls us o'er the tumult
Of our life's wild, restless sea;

Day by day His sweet voice soundeth,
Saying, "Christian, follow Me."

Jesus calls us from the worship
Of the vain world's golden store,
From each idol that would keep us,
Saying, "Christian, love Me more."

In our joys and in our sorrows,
Days of toil and hours of ease,
Still He calls in cares and pleasures,
"Christian, love Me more than these."

Jesus calls us: by Thy mercies,
Savior, may we hear Thy call,
Give our hearts to Thine obedience,
Serve and love Thee best of all.[2]

And then, Oswald was gone.

November 15, 1917, not quite six months after Biddy spent her seventh wedding anniversary with her husband, Mrs. Oswald Chambers was a widow. She was thirty-three years old.

In our telephone conversations, Kathleen had told me how Biddy handled the sudden loss of Oswald. She explained to me that God's Word sustained her mother. She knew there was no permanent good-bye. To believe in God meant that Biddy had to decide for herself not to let her heart be troubled. At a time like that, faith is a reality, not a pie-in-the-sky idea.

Kathleen said, "My mother didn't understand at first, and she wondered why he died when she was sure that the sickness was not to be unto death but for the glory of God. But later my mother realized that God's purposes were always good. Her sense of loss was made a cause to rejoice as she went forward to do God's will. She knew that God would make it plain to her each step of the way. She felt God's assurance because Jesus Christ was the foundation."

When Oswald Chambers was suddenly taken into God's presence, Biddy Chambers knew that crying would not empty her heart of pain. Her choice was clear. Sitting alone on a rough wooden bench in the devotional hut in Zeitoun, Egypt, in November 1917, she could still hear Oswald teaching the soldiers. He promised them that if they chose to follow Jesus Christ, they would receive life eternal.

About three weeks later, alone for a few minutes in the devotional hut, Biddy Chambers sat quietly reading Oswald's Bible. She felt close to him then. He was just beyond the veil, with Jesus.

She did not, however, expect to come across a letter he had written in October 1917 to the former students of the Bible Training College.

Amazed at her discovery, she sat back on the hard wooden chair at her study table and read his cheery message, which reminded them that the true source of life, Jesus Christ, would keep them strong as they trusted him for each day. He admonished them to allow God to order their circumstances, to concentrate on their personal relationship with Jesus, and above all, to know that B.T.C., "Better To Come," was still their watchword. She felt the presence of Christ in a very real way.

"Mrs. O. C.?"

A young man dressed in military uniform hesitated at the doorway to the hut.

"Yes?" Startled, Biddy smiled.

"May I come in?" He held his hat in his hands.

"Yes, yes, of course. Please do." Biddy gestured toward a roughly hewn wooden chair not too far from the study table.

"I've been wondering." He fumbled with his hat and lowered his eyes so that she could not see his tears.

"Yes? What is it?" Biddy Chambers's heart went out to him. She could feel his grief.

"How will we go on without a teacher?" His lower lip quivered, but he straightened his shoulders to hear her reply.

"Well," Biddy replied calmly, acting as if she did not see his distress, "we shall simply learn the truths of God together. As we keep his Word, he will keep us!"

Turning to the book of Psalms, she read out loud,

> I will lift up mine eyes unto the hills, from whence cometh my help. My help cometh from the LORD, which made heaven and earth. He will not suffer thy foot to be moved: he that keepeth thee will not slumber. Behold, he that keepeth Israel shall neither slumber nor sleep. The LORD is thy keeper: the LORD is thy shade upon thy right hand. The sun shall not smite thee by day, nor the moon by night. The LORD shall preserve thee from all evil: he shall preserve thy soul. The LORD shall preserve thy going out and thy coming in from this time forth, and even for evermore.   PSALM 121:1-8 (KJV)

That was the beginning of God's order, even in the seemingly haphazard, for the messages of Oswald Chambers to reach around the world.

Biddy's loving response to the grief shared by so many was to make certain her notes got into print. Loving hands of others helped get the printings out to the men up and down the battle line. Like clockwork, each month a talk was transcribed into writing, printed, and sent to all those eagerly waiting for encouragement.

By 1918, the Y.M.C.A. had assumed the responsibility of printing and distributing the material.

Meanwhile, also in 1918, Germany signed an armistice with the Allies, bringing an end to the First World War.

The Great War had killed millions. Some estimate that at least twenty million others were blinded, maimed, mutilated, and crippled. Others were permanently disabled by shell shock. No one really knows for certain how many were lost, but World War I had an impact on virtually the entire globe.

Civilians as well as soldiers lost their lives under horrific conditions.

Where was God in this? He was right there, and for all who would ask, Jesus took them home. "Everyone who asks, receives; all who seek, find; and the door is opened to everyone who knocks" (Luke 11:10, TLB).

When May of 1919 rolled around, one of Oswald's talks that had been given in Zeitoun in the devotional hut was printed, and ten thousand copies were distributed among the camps in Palestine and Egypt and friends in France.

Oswald's life was best celebrated by others carrying on his work after his death.

During all of these events, the blackboard still had daily words written for the men at Zeitoun, and enthusiasm for the task at hand was high.

Requests for more material arrived daily. Biddy just kept transcribing notes and doing her daily duties, and Kathleen chattered happily as she rode on her small donkey and continued to acquire more pets for Biddy to love.

Then, in July 1919, God brought the time in Egypt to an end.

Biddy Chambers, a young widow, returned home to England with little Kathleen to face what was left of her world.

"Hi, Kathleen. How's the heat wave in London? I heard about it on the news last night."

"Hot." Kathleen chuckled, then coughed.

"Are you sick?" I asked.

"Just a bit of bronchitis. The air isn't very good right now. Lady doesn't like it either. She's just lying around a lot."

"Dogs are smarter about the weather than we are," I replied quickly. "Cookie says 'woof' to Lady. So, are you up to one big question?"

"How big?" Kathleen coughed again.

"If you're not well enough . . ."

"Just let me get a drink of water."

While Kathleen went for a glass of water, I tried to prepare my question so it wouldn't seem as long as it was.

"I'm back."

"Great! Here goes . . . I know that your mother, in addition to everything else, was a capable businesswoman, especially after you all returned to England. She took in university students and boarders during the day and typed your father's words at night, right?"

"Right."

"Just let me know if you need to hang up." Kathleen was so good to me that my heart hurt to think of her sitting in the heat and trying not to cough.

"I will."

"Promise?"

"Yes," she warmly responded. "Give it your best shot."

"Okay. Good. Thanks. Your mother went home to

heaven January 15, 1966. That made her eighty-three years old, right?"

"Yes."

"Following are some thoughts I have about your mother, and I will send you a copy, too, so that you can correct me where it is necessary:

- What kind of a woman would give up her freedom to commit herself to a man who had no job, no place to live, and a shaky future?
- What makes a woman follow a man, literally, to the ends of the earth and play hostess to thousands of troubled soldiers?
- What woman could gracefully feed from one extra person to twenty or more when she wasn't even certain what was for dinner except guests?
- What kind of woman could live underground to escape sweltering sunshine and not complain?
- What kind of woman could lose all that she had—the man she had given her life to, the security of family love—in an instant, and not lose her way in the face of overwhelming grief?
- What kind of woman could go on to raise their only daughter in poverty?
- What kind of woman would be able to work long hours, from sunup to sundown, and then proceed to begin her "real" work at the end of the day, transcribing the notes of her dead husband into words that others could read?
- What kind of woman could face each day of uncertainty with confidence in God?

"That is all one question?" Kathleen laughed out loud, but she didn't cough, and I was happy about that. I heard Lady barking in the background.

"Lady has to go?"

"Yes. I will send you a poem I wrote about my mother. It may answer your question."

"I didn't know you write poetry!"

"Just a little." Just then, Lady became louder and more persistent.

Not too many days afterward, Kathleen sent me the poem she had written about her mother. She wrote,

Not merely in the words you say
Not only in the deeds confessed
But in the most unconscious way
It is expressed.
Is it a beatific smile?
A holy light upon the brow?
Oh no, I felt his Presence while
You laughed just now.
For me was not the truth you taught
To you so clear to me still dim
But when you came to me you brought
A sense of him
And from your eyes he beckoned me
And from your heart his love is shed
Till I lose sight of you and see
The Christ instead.

  —ANONYMOUS

Then she added, "Keep your chin up and your tail wagging! All will be well, I'm sure. Much love to you. It is good that you have the book about my mother in your heart. Love from Lady to your small dog, Cookie. Love and God bless you, Kathleen."

Tears welled in my eyes as I read. "How like her to sign it 'Anonymous,'" I said to Cookie.

With all humility and full of God's love, Kathleen had given me the answer to her mother's secret life, one hidden with Christ in God. Biddy Chambers, like her husband, Oswald Chambers, followed Jesus Christ.

Not long after that, I received an announcement that on May 30, 1997, Kathleen Chambers had joined her mother and father in heaven at the age of eighty-four.

I felt very alone in my grief at Kathleen's passing, but because of what I had learned from her, I knew I was not alone. God was with me. Kathleen would want me to love him most of all.

For all the blossoms trying to bloom in this earthly garden, Kathleen Chambers taught me that joy comes in the morning and that morning always comes. Like the rose and the daffodil, we weather storms, sunshine, and rain, but the Son shines forever.

PILOGUE

In my diary I wrote the following: "Biddy Chambers trusted God. Because she trusted God, millions of her husband's words have found their way into sorrowing souls to take root and grow into a very personal relationship with Jesus Christ. She wrote our way to peace."

For us, as believers in Jesus Christ, there is no end. We'll see each other again.

I can hardly wait.

Notes

Chapter 3

1. John Wesley (1703–1791), *A Collection of Hymns for the Use of the People Called Methodists* (London: Wesleyan Conference Office, 1877).

2. George Matheson (1842–1906), "O Love That Will Not Let Me Go," in *The One Year Great Songs of Faith* (Carol Stream, IL: Tyndale, 2005), 71.

Chapter 5

1. D. A. Lincoln, *Boston Cooking School Cook Book* (Boston: Roberts Brothers, 1884), republished in 1996 by Dover Publications, Mineola, New York.

Chapter 6

1. "Royal Arsenal," http://en.wikipedia.org/wiki/Royal_Arsenal.

Chapter 7

1. Miles J. Stanford, "Oswald Chambers," www.withchrist.org/MJS.

2. I am indebted to the Wesley Center Online, Northwest Nazarene University, Nampa, ID 83686 for permission to quote from Ian M. Randall, "The Pentecostal League of Prayer: A Transdenominational British Wesleyan-Holiness Movement," *Wesleyan Theological*

Journal 33, no. 1 (Spring 1998), http://wesley.nnu.edu/
wesleyan_theology/theojrnl/31-35/33-1-10.htm.

3. J. Ford, *In the Steps of John Wesley: The Church of the Nazarene in Britain* (Kansas City, MO: 1968), 91.

4. M. R. Hooker, *Adventures of an Agnostic* (London, 1959), 112.

5. http://wesley.nnu.edu/wesleyan_theology/theojrnl/31-35-33-1-10.htm. Accessed October 10, 2007.

6. Keith Drury, "The Holiness Movement: Dead or Alive?" Dennis Bratcher, ed. http://www.crivoice.org/hmovement.html. Accessed October 10, 2007.

Chapter 8

1. Arabella Catherine (Kate) Hankey (1834–1911), "I Love to Tell the Story" in *The One Year Great Songs of Faith* (Carol Stream, IL: Tyndale, 2005), 167.

2. Samuel John Stone (1839–1900), "The Church's One Foundation," in *The One Year Great Songs of Faith* (Carol Stream, IL: Tyndale, 2005), 238.

Chapter 9

1. "Oswald Chambers," http://www.wheaton.edu/learnres/ARCSC/collects/sc122/bio.htm.

2. "Family—Family Problems." http://www.vysokeskoly.cz/maturitniotazky/otazky/anglictina/Family.htm. Accessed October 10, 2007.

3. "When Morning Gilds the Skies," in *The One Year Great Songs of Faith* (Carol Stream, IL: Tyndale, 2005), 222. Translated from *Katholisches Gesangbuch* (Würtzburg, Germany, 1828). Stanzas 1, 2, and 4 were translated by Edward Caswall (1814–1878). Stanza 3 was translated by Robert Seymour Bridges (1844–1930).

Chapter 10

1. *Merriam-Webster's Collegiate Dictionary,* 11th ed., s.v. "nest."

2. Walter Chalmers Smith, "Immortal, Invisible, God Only Wise," in *The One Year Great Songs of Faith* (Carol Stream, IL: Tyndale, 2005), 193. The hymn was first published in 1876 in *Hymns of Christ and Christian Life.* The text was later altered by Walter Smith and was published 1884 in W. Garrett Horder's *Congregational Hymns.*

Chapter 12

1. Henry Francis Lyte, "Abide with Me" in *The One Year Great Songs of Faith* (Carol Stream, IL: Tyndale, 2005), 28. Lyte was born in Scotland in 1793 and wrote the words in 1847, just three weeks before his death from tuberculosis.

Chapter 13

1. Harriet Beecher Stowe (1812–1896), "Still, Still with Thee," http://cyberhymnal.org/htm/s/t/stilstil.htm. Based on the words from Psalm 139:18: "When I wake up, you are still with me!" (NLT).

Chapter 14

1. *Merriam-Webster's Collegiate Dictionary,* 11th ed., s.v. "lady."

2. Cecil Frances Alexander (1818–1895), "Jesus Calls Us," in *The One Year Great Songs of Faith* (Carol Stream, IL: Tyndale, 2005), 299.